# *Dedication*

This book is dedicated to my good friend, ally, and neighbor, Sam Butcher.

With out tight schedules both of us busy building our dreams, his being the Precious Moments Chapel and mine being Red Oak II, and all the while trying to up with out dedicated collectors. We didn't get to spend as much time together as we would have liked, but, Sam has a sixth sense about things, and seems to know when I am hurting the most, or having major problems in my life and career, or if something else is wrong.

He was in the Philippines the first time I suffered a deep depression while I was on the road touring and he just sensed it, that far away, and called Charlie and asked her if there was anything he could do.

Sam has been there for me, helping me financially with my projects, in the building of Red Oak II, without ever asking for anything in return.

He was there the second time I lost it and torched my studio. I could go on and on about all the times Sam has been there for me.

I loved it when Sam and I could get together and how excited he got showing me his latest paintings, showing us around the Chapel, the grounds, and his latest additions, like The Fountain of Angels.

I understand completely because I get the same excitement and enthusiasm when I show him my latest paintings or any new acquisitions that I had made in Red Oak II.

There is no one else that I know of who has done so much for this area and for Carthage as you have Sam. You have given generously and graciously to the arts, the churches, the schools, and to individuals in need.

Thank You Sam! Thanx for being my friend.

P.S. One of the best things for me was Sam moving to Carthage, Missouri, as it used to be when a stranger or collector drove in town they would ask a local resident, "Where does that crazy artist live?" Now that Sam lives here, the locals ask the out-of-towners, "Which one?"

A SPECIAL THANKS

If I would have had enough interest in spelling, and trying to remember my spelling words in grade school, I'm sure this book would have been easier to edit. Instead of cheating by writing my spelling words on the bottom of my shoe, it would have been easier for me to write this book.

If I had paid more attention in my English classes, I wouldn't have needed Miss Dallie quite as much as I have during the long writing process.

I didn't have a computer, word processor, or even a typewriter when I started this project. All I ever used as a word processor was a Big Chief tablet and a #2 lead pencil. For Miss Dallie to make heads or tails out of my hen scratch and for it to be readable and make sense, I give a special thanks to Miss Dallie Miessner of Howerton.

*Other Titles by Lowell Davis*

The Sheldon and Blossom
Coloring Book

The Book on Chickens
Pelican Publishing Company
Gretna, 1998

## Table of Contents

Chapter 1 -- The Early Years ------------------------------------------------- 1

Chapter 2 -- My Pierre Days ------------------------------------------------- 20

Chapter 3 -- Charlie ------------------------------------------------------- 30

Chapter 4 -- The Farm ------------------------------------------------------ 38

Chapter 5 -- Schmid, the good years, the Leapin' Lizard --------------------- 49

Chapter 6 -- Red Oak II ---------------------------------------------------- 58

Chapter 7 -- The Demise of Schmid ------------------------------------------ 61

Chapter 8 -- The Farm Club ------------------------------------------------- 71

Chapter 9 -- Finding my Niche, I thought ----------------------------------- 76

Chapter 10 -- My Darkest Days ---------------------------------------------- 83

Chapter 11 -- Rose, The new beginning -------------------------------------- 86

Postscript ----------------------------------------------------------------- 91

## *About The Author*

Lowell Davis, the man, was born in a small hamlet in southwestern Missouri, named Red Oak, that is no longer on the map, if indeed it ever was.

It is said that God grants all creatures a talent which allows them to survive in life. When God looked upon Lowell Davis, he kind of smiled and figured since Lowell was such a country kid he would need more than average talent, so God blessed him with an abundance.

Literally millions of people have been enthralled with his art work in the form of paintings, sculptures of farm animal figurines, toys and collectables of all God's creatures found on the woodlands around the world. Most people never dream of possessing the talent this man has, yet he continues to amaze us with expanding his horizons to now include writing.

His first book, a coloring book written for elementary school children featured two of his masterpiece figurines brought to life by his brilliant illustrations in the form of a coloring book that emphasizes acceptance of children with physical and mental challenges. The Sheldon and Blossom Coloring Book was passed out to school children in southwest Missouri for over twenty years.

His second book, *"The Book on Chickens"* is a delightfully funny insight into the life of farm animals during their everyday lives on the farm. Totally illustrated with Lowell's original art, the book is a dozen laughs on every page.

This current work, "there ain't no memories in First Class" is a short autobiographical look into the life of one of America's most brilliant artists.

It is a refreshing look at a man that has a higher esteem for his roots than desire for monetary gain; a deeper affection for his childhood home than the mansions wealth can bring and a happiness that only a walk with God can bring.

Thank you for sharing this with us Lowell.

Your friend,
Thomas Nabors
December 2005

# *Acknowledgements*

I always keep in mind, never snob anyone while climbing the ladder of success because you have to face many of those same people on the way down.

There are far too many people that have helped me during my life and career that it would be impossible to thank all of them here, so, I'll just single out a few that has helped with the publication of this book.

I would like to offer a special gratitude Sam Butcher and JoJo who treated me as royalty on my visit to the Philippines and made my visit both entertaining and life altering.

And of course, it is equally important that I acknowledge the contribution and support of my dear friends Darrell and Larrene Hagaman of Webb City, Missouri.

Larrene for playing cupid and Darrell for tying the knot. Their friendship and support is so very deeply appreciated. I want to thank my Florida friend Dale Abbott, who for the love of my art, paid to have this book published.

I no longer have a mother, Miss Metsker or my Aunt Deloris to brag on me, so I want to thank my friend Thomas Nabors. He has spent hundreds of donated hours editing, typing, and finalizing this book plus all those flowery words in the About the Author section.

The list goes on, you all know who you are, and thanks again.

Your friend;
Lowell Davis

# *Introduction*

It never ceases to amaze me the nicknames people acquire throughout their lives. Somehow, most of them seem to fit the people upon which they are pinned. In the case of Lowell Davis, this has never been more true.

He was called Pierre in his younger days because he his behind the pseudonym as he was afraid his art would not be good enough and he did not wish to embarrass his family. The name fit because he kind of reminds me of an artist you might see sitting at some small Paris café painting his heart out, only Lowell would be wearing blue jeans, a bandana as a cravat and smoking his ever present corn cob pipe.

Later, since he was country when country wasn't cool, he would be called the "father of country art". And still later he would be called the "Norman Rockwell of rural art". Lowell even refers to himself by a seldom used, but very endeared nickname. To him and those close to him, he is simply the "Missoura Kid". If Lowell could be reincarnated as a cartoon character he would come back to us as Missoura Kid.

But to me he is simply "the Wiz!" I think of him as the Wiz because of his awesome talent. Yes, I am so tired of hearing the term "awesome" used so often to elevate the mundane to a level of divinity; however, in the case of Lowell Davis' skill with a pencil, a paint brush, a carving tool, or just simple conversation, the only term that fits is "awesome". He is a living marvel.

While assisting him bring this book from the ashes of memory to the written word I have had the pleasure of spending many hours in his company. I, a person not easily impressed by mankind, continue to be awed in his presence. He is the kindest and most gentle person I have ever met. He is a true country gentleman and the most generous with his talent, his time, and his delightful wit.

Reading this short autobiographical account on his life, thought it is not an in depth work, is a delightful and entertaining peek into his charm, wit, and loving character. You will laugh a little and if like me, cry a little. You will sink in the pond as low as his wedding ring and fly as high as the Guardian Angels that are ever present watching over him.

Enjoy the words of the man and envision with him the hopes and dreams of a country boys efforts to save a small town from extinction.

After you have finished, take a few moments to go to his web site at http://lowelldavis-artist.com and enjoy hundreds of his drawings, paintings and sculpted figurines.

Thomas Nabors.
December 2005

Lowell Davis

# Chapter 1

# ON A JUNE NIGHT

**Farm where Lowell was born**

## THE EARLY YEARS:

It was in an upstairs bedroom on an old farm house that I took my first breath; a beautiful June night during cherry pickin' time. The doctor charged my parents $10.00 dollars to deliver me and many times during my growing up years I think my Mama considered asking for her money back.

Times were real tough that year of 1937. Not only was there a full fledged depression going on, but the dust bowl was in full swing and thousands of people were packing up and heading to California with hopes of a better life. My Dad had his dreams too and shortly after my birth he sold the farm and had an auction.

Dad began moving, roaming from place to place. He blamed his wanderlust on the weather and on all the dust and drought, but I think it was his love for the west and his yearning to just start roving. He never got tied down again or bought another piece of property until I was in the fifth grade.

After the sale Dad built a trailer and pulled it behind out 1940 Ford sedan and moved us to Red Oak, Missouri. Then we moved to Rescue, Missouri, where he ran a garage on old Route 66.

We lived in a lot of places in and around Red Oak. We moved from one house to another, but each year we made a trip to Colorado or California.

When we lived in California, Dad worked in an orange packing plant for the Santa Fe Railroad. Then, we'd move back to Red Oak again, run the General Store, and live in the back of the store. Later, we'd pack up our belongings and move to Colorado and Dad would do different jobs. He blamed his health as the reason for wanting to live in the west, but I think it was more that he just loved the west, but the time we moved to a little mining town on top of a mountain near Canyon City, Colorado was the beginning of the end of those wandering years for Dad. It was the last straw for Mom.

Dad worked in a mine and we occupied one of the three mining shacks on the property. It was hard. We didn't even have inside plumbing. Finally Mom said, "Berton, no more!" It was the first time I had ever heard Mom put her foot down. In fact, I never heard my Mom and Dad argue, although I do remember Dad going outside a lot of times and mowing the lawn. Even when it didn't need mowed, or in the winter.

After that, we moved to Red Oak for the last time. Again Dad operated the General Store for my uncle Clair Easson and we lived in the back of the store. Of all the places we lived, Red Oak was my favorite.

Now, Red Oak was a small farming community snuggled in the foothills of the Ozark Mountains. It consisted of the General Store, my great-grandpa W. W. Weber's blacksmith's shop, a Methodist Church, the IOOF lodge, a country school, the Mason's Lodge, and my uncle Clair Easson's Oliver dealership. There were also about thirty houses plus all the farm houses that dotted the countryside and one set of great-grandparents. In fact, my great-great-grandparents, Clyman, on my mother's side, were among the first white settlers in this area to put a plow in the ground.

My dad's side of the family moved to the Red Oak area in the early 1920's.

All of u shared close family ties and I sure enjoyed playing with my cousins and visiting my uncles and aunts on their farms. It was a good thing I had a lot of cousins, aunts, uncles, grandparents, not to mention my older brother Ivan and his wife Dorothy.

I would spend my summer vacations going from one relative's farm to another. I would spend a week at one relative's until they got sick of me, then I'd go spend a week at another relative's house. It was fortunate I had many relations with farms in the vicinity so they didn't have to put up with me twice in one summer.

Red Oak was a self sufficient community with neighbors helping neighbors. Everyone had their own gardens, their own Jersey cows, and we had a small edge up on my cousins and the other neighbor kids because most of our clothes were made from feed sacks, and in those days, all the feed came in cotton sacks with printed patterns on them. And as we lived in the back of the General Store, I was right there to get first choice. I had to make sure they didn't have flowers printed on them.

We didn't notice the depression that much because all the families in the Red Oak area had about the same lifestyle we did. All we had to buy was coffee, sugar, cereal, salt, and a few items like that. Everyone was poor, we just didn't know it. In fact, I didn't know I was poor until I moved to Carthage and they told me I was poor.

**A young Lowell Davis and Subject**

## BECOMING AN ARTIST:

My love of painting began at an early age. When I dumped out my first box of crayons and make a few scribbles, I knew I wanted to become an artist. In fact, my mom said I painted my first mural when I was two years old. Yep! She just kept moving my crib around the room.

My parents and relatives, all from farm backgrounds, didn't understand how anyone could make a living as an artist.

I tell a lot of folks that knew me when I was a little kid, I didn't want to work for a living, that's why I wanted to become an artist.

There wasn't much of a chance to get exposure to art in Red Oak. I guess that's why I was always so excited when the *"Saturday Evening Post"* arrived at the General Store. I studied it like a Bible. First, I would look at the cover, hoping there would be a Norman Rockwell painting. (That's when Norman Rockwell became my hero). Then I went through the magazine looking and studying the cartoons. Little did I know that one day, many years later, a story about me would be featured in the *"Saturday Evening Post"*.

Much of my education was from the old timers who gathered at he General Store. In the winter they sat around the old pot-bellied stove and on the front porch in the summer. They would whittle and tell yarns. I was always in awe of these characters, and as a kid, I would sit by the hour and listen to them and watch them whittle.

The only person who supported my dreams and understood them was my grandpa Clyman. He was a Jack of all trades, a carpenter, a mason, and a musician. He could even draw a little bit. He taught me what he knew. I know he mainly did it to keep my interest in art alive.

As a student at Red Oak country school, I wasn't much at reading, writing and arithmetic, but when it came to cutting out Santa Clauses, turkeys and Easter bunnies, well, that was where I really shined.

The best part of the school day was "story time". That's when the teacher read to us from the books and my absolute favorites were the Uncle Remus stories. My imagination ran wild with the goings on of Brer rabbit, Tar Baby and all the other Remus characters.

**The Davis family moving west**

## GROWING UP:

The summer before I entered the fifth grade, my dad finally decided to settle down. We moved to Carthage, Missouri. A large town of eleven thousand people back then, and twenty three miles west of Red Oak on old Route 66.

Although Dad's roaming days were over and he'd settled down, it didn't mean he didn't still love the west. Even when he was at home in his easy chair, he would entertain himself for hours just dreaming and studying maps.

He had a little syrup can, shaped like a log cabin, in which he saved his dimes all during the year. Those dimes would be our gas money on out trips to Colorado and to California the next summer when we'd visit Aunt Deloris, Uncle Lenville, and Aunt Betty and Uncle J.D. Dad always tried to take a different route each time we drove west, and always my favorite route was old Route 66. I think a lot of my love for that old highway was watching the changing on the countryside as we drove by. During those years Route 66 went right smack dab through the middle of every town, large and small, between Missoura and California.

The scenery was very different in those days. There was no such thing as chain food restaurants or any other business chains. Almost all of the businesses on the old 66 were Mom and Pop places, where the owners lived in back of their stores. What fascinated me the most about these places was the way they enticed people to pull off the road and trade with them. I loved the different ways they promoted and advertised their businesses, the art work and the lettering they used.

The further west we went, the signs would keep changing as would the architecture of the little places of business. When we reached New Mexico, the houses and stores were mostly made of adobe. This was a drastic style of art work, but I remember, even so long ago, every bit of it. They did the best they could with what they had to work with. They didn't take short cuts. Those people made art out of work. I always recognize anyone that builds something, does lettering, lays stone, whatever they do, and do it the very best of their ability, as artists. An artist's medium doesn't have to be only water colors, oil, or clay.

Art work and lettering, I think, were my favorite things to do as I sat in the back seat with my brother Ivan, and my sister, Evelyn.

I loved to watch the countryside go by, so I always conned them into letting me sit by the window. I could ride for hours, watching and studying the different architecture of the Mom and Pop paces along the side of the highway and the way that their individuality gave them their distinct personality. Today, American Architecture has sold itself down the drain, for convenience. Whatever are the easiest and most convenient, that's what they go for.

I also loved the different style of architecture in the little one room school houses, churches, farms and farmhouses along the route. Just as the landscape changed, the road signs and building materials changed just as drastically.

Through the Oklahoma panhandle and Texas, the siding on most of the buildings was made of their native stone or clapboard. This began my fascination with stone mason's and their art. When we got into New Mexico, their places of business turned into adobe. Then construction would change into log as you got into the higher elevations of Arizona. All of these places had their owner's personalities.

My absolute favorites were the animal zoos. These were usually at little gas stations that dotted old 66 through the desert areas of Arizona and California. They had hand painted signs, advertising for miles before you approached their places of business.
Signs like, "See rattle snakes – coyotes – Gila monsters", and whatever animal or reptile indigenous to the desert.

I would beg Dad to fill up the car at the stations with free zoos in the back of their establishments. As the station owner was filling up the car with gas, my family and I would enter through the tall wooden fence that was the free entrance. We would walk through and see the prairie dog town. Cougars, bobcat, and coyotes were in small cages that the proprietor built out of whatever materials they happened to have on hand.

Always, as we were exiting the free zoo there was a donation pail. The attendant hurried to fill our car with gas and would be standin' by the donation pail with a big smile as he asked how we enjoyed the zoo. Dad would dig down in his pocket for some of those hard earned dimes and would drop them so the attendant could hear the plunk of coins hitting the bottom of the pail.

Today, as I drove over that same old route, none of those little masterpieces are in business. Mostly the little Mom and Pop places have been torn down and replaces with new "all-look-alike" businesses that are usually made up of "all-look-alike" chain stores. Every little grocery store and gas station is a chain on some kind of "git and go" with absolutely zero personality.

Now every business looks the same. You can't tell one street corner in one town from a street corner in another town. In fact, you can't tell Oklahoma from Arizona or New Mexico from California. They just don't have the same charm. The new places of business are absolutely tasteless. The art factor is blatantly void.

Even when Dad wasn't driving out west, and was sitting at home in his easy chair, he would entertain me for hours with stories of his ventures in the west, and of course, he always told me about the time he, and his brother and their dad, went to California in a model-T Ford looking for work during the "Grapes of Wrath" era.

**Forged in Fire mural Lowell painted in the Jasper County Courthouse**

# CARTHAGE:

When we moved to Carthage, Dad bought one of those Mom and Pop types of gas stations on the south side of town. It was a little station where we sold gas and a few groceries and our family lived in the back of the store. Dad build a "man and woman" outside privy which served our family's needs and our customer's too.

I loved to hang around the station. I hand pumped the gas and talked to the customers, most of the tourists that were heading to some far away destination. I was always fascinated by their stories.

Right next store to my dad's little business lived a young couple that operated a frosty type ice cream establishment. The man was a hobby artist and did a few watercolors. I was fascinated by him, mainly because he was the first real bonafide artist I had ever met. I know I pestered tat man to death asking him questions about art and buggin' him to teach me how to paint with watercolors. He gave me an old Prang water color box and a few of his old, used brushes and showed me the basics of applying watercolors. Up to that point my only art medium was a Big Chief tablet and a #2 pencil.

My neighbor was a landscape painter and taught me how to pain trees and water. After my second painting, I thought, "Look out Norman Rockwell, here I come."

One day as we were going through some of his sketch books, we ran across a little water color sketch of his beautiful young wife, posed in the nude. After that, every time I was in their living quarters if he wasn't looking, I would flip through his sketch book until I came to the page with the nude, and I would sit and study it. I always knew I wanted to be an artist, but it was at the ripe old age of eleven that I decided that I wanted to be a nude artist.

I dabbled in watercolors for a couple of years, along with my constant sketching and drawing cartoons. It seemed I was always in trouble with my grade school teachers because I would draw cartoons and doodle all over my books. When they scolded me, my answer was always, "Yeah, teacher , but this is the way I take notes." I could look through my drawings and tell them what they were talking about just by looking at those doodles. My teachers didn't buy that explanation and made me pay for the books I had drawn all over, but I still kept doodling and drawing cartoons all over my books, knowing that someday I would be a world-famous cartoonist.

The Christmas I was in the fifth grade I was walking around the public square in Carthage. Just off the square was Gilbrath's, a paint and wallpaper store that carried a minimum amount of art supplies.

Well, there it was, just before Christmas, and as I looked into their front window I saw a little oil painting set in a redwood box. It had fourteen small tubes of Grumbaucher oil paints and about six different style and shapes of brushes, a small bottle of turpentine and a small bottle of linseed oil, and a pallet – all of that for only $14.00 dollars.

At the supper table that night, I excitedly told my folks about the box of oil paints. At that time, my parents really didn't understand art or why I wanted to be an artist, but as poor as they were, my dad managed to scrape up enough money to have it wrapped up for me and under the Christmas tree.

When I opened my package that Christmas morning and found those oil pains I wanted to get started on my art career. I found myself a piece of paper, then took my mother's old print of a mountain scene off the wall, sat down with my freshly squeezed array of colors on my palette, and reproduced that mountain scene on a piece of paper. I had to use paper as dad couldn't afford to buy me canvas, too.

As soon as I opened that bottle of turpentine and took a whiff of it – the turpentine entered my bloodstream. From that day on, I knew my medium would be oil paints.

The next year I painted on everything I could get my hands on. I painted on pine boards and my dad would bring home little pieces of Masonite from his carpenter's job site. He would prime the Masonite with white house paint and I would use them in lieu of canvas. I also painted on drinking glasses and dishes.

I painted like this until I entered the sixth grade. My teacher that year was Miss Metsker, who saw the spark of talent that was burning inside of me. At that time there was only one art teacher in Carthage, Nell Esterly, who have art lessons in her home on Saturdays. Miss Metsker asked if I wanted to take art lessons from Mrs. Esterly, if she could arrange it for me. I told her I would rather do that than anything in the world, and I also told her my folks could barely keep me in brushes and tubes of paint, much less ever come up with the fifty cents each Saturday that Mrs. Esterly charged for lessons.

Miss Metsker said, "Lowell, you let me worry about paying for the lessons." She paid for me art lessons throughout my grade school years.

I remember my years at Mark Twain grade school. I was always staring out the window. My body was in that class room, but my mind was outdoors in the woods or wandering off to far away places. I remember taking history, English and arithmetic, all the time thinking, "why do I need to learn all this crap, anyways? I'm going to be an artist and why in the world would an artist need to know a pronoun from an adjective?"

So, with this attitude, I made very poor grades in school. I had Miss Metsker for two years and during those two years I painter for her hoping this might get me a few brownie points so she would pass me on to high school.

I painted her a large oil of Washington Crossing the Delaware, a large painting of the signing tower in Florida (her favorite building), and a small oil of Thomas Jefferson's home, Monticello.

Then I did a pastel, or color chalk rendering of the Hermitage, Andrew Jackson's home in Nashville, Tennessee, that covered an entire section of the blackboard in her class room. She never allowed it to be removed. In fact, it stayed there for the duration of her teaching career. I even went back to Mark Twain after I got out of the Air Force and it was still there. I found out that if any student ever molested, or ran their finger though that sketch, it was almost a death sentence in her class.

**Lowell's first painting for his mother**

In the sixth grade, a friend and my classmates nicknamed me "Pierre". I don't know if it was the little French beret I war to school, my wanting to be an artist, or if it was because I was a lover, or all the above.

Back in those growing up years, I knew I wanted to be an artist and I used different pseudonyms when signing my paintings. Sometimes I signed them Jerry Davis, Pierre Davis, or Marchand, which was an old family name. My reason is that I was so vain I didn't want my real name, Lowell Davis, on all those practice paintings. I wasn't going to use my real name until I figured I had mastered my medium.

Being the best artist in your school class or Sunday school meant that if there was any lettering or poster art that came up, you were assigned to do it, and I didn't mind a bit. It was either that or studying and sometimes my teachers would pass me through their class just to get rid of me.

I passed all my grades that way until my sophomore year in high school. That year was the first time I ever received any type of art course that was taught in the public school system. However, my art teacher was a football coach who substituted as an art teacher. I failed art and English that year. I know why I failed English – complete lack of interest. I think the reason I failed art was that I told the football coach/art teacher that I knew more about art in my little finger than he knew about art in his whole body. I think that pissed him off because he gave me an "F" in art.

At the time, I didn't worry much about finishing high school, so I quit at the end of my sophomore year. Anyway, I had places to go, things to do, and people to meet. I wanted to get outta this podunk town of Carthage, anyway.

**Oil painting of Lowell's C-119 over Europe**

## THE AIR FORCE:

The summer of 1954, was one of the hottest on record, and it was in August of that year that I decided to join the Air Force. It was like jumping from the frying pan into the fire. I was sent to Lackland Air Force Base in San Antonio, Texas, where it was much hotter than it was at home.

After I completed my basic training I was given three choices of what I wanted to do. I put down artist, air police, or a cook. I didn't get any of the above as the Air Force thought they needed ground radio operators.

After basic training, I was sent to Keesler Air Force Base in Biloxi, Mississippi, and trained as a ground radio operator. The only art exposure I got while stationed there was that on weekends I would catch a bus bound for New Orleans. In New Orleans there were always artists hanging around painting at Rembrandt Square. So, at night I hit the bars and strip joints on Bourbon Street and during the day I watched artists paint. After six months at Keeler I was shipped to England.

Already I had been to two of the far off places I had dreamed about as O stared out my classroom window, San Antonio and New Orleans. Now I was headed for England..

My first assignment was supposed to be at Burtonwood Air Force Base in England, but when I got there and checked in they looked at my records and said, "there must be some mistake." They didn't even use ground radio operators at that base, so, they transferred me to Rhine/Main Air Force Base at Frankfort, Germany.

Again, upon arrival I was told, "nope, we don't have any vacancies for ground radio operators." Then I was sent to Evereux, France. Now I was seeing Europe just from going from one Air Force base to another.

When I got to Evereux, the same ole thing, ground radio operators were becoming obsolete, but I was told the had an opening for an airborne radio operator. "Would I be willing to transfer my job description to airborne?" I said "sure", and jumped at the chance.

Now, with a crash course, converting from ground to airborne, I was flying with the "big dogs". I was assigned to a cargo and paratrooper type squad that flew C-119's with a four man crew: the pilot, the co-pilot, the crew chief and radio operator.

I loved it. Here I was, barely 18 years old, and was flying to every country in Europe and all over Africa. It was a great experience for a young man who dreamed of seeing the world.

At the time, it was ten years after World War II. Most of Europe had recovered and rebuilt from the destruction of the war and all the charm of the old Europe still remained. There were no skyscrapers in the big cities of Rome, Paris, or London. Big European cities in those days still had their old culture, steam trains, and horses pulling carts in the villages, still farming mostly with work horses. It was all like candy to my eyes. I was trying to soak up as much of it as my young eyes could absorb.

**Photo of Airman Davis, circa: Way back when**

I didn't dabble much in art those first two years in Europe. I was more interested in how many girls I could impress in my flight suit, the red beret we wore, my spit-shined jump boots, and the white scarf we all kept tucked in out flight suits. I was sure pretty, and cocky!

As soon as we landed in different towns and cities in the different countries the crew chief and I would hit the bars at night. I couldn't tell you anything about Rome's Colosseum, but I could tell you the name of every bar in Rome. I never went to the great museums in London, but I could tell you about all the bars in Amsterdam, Paris, Lisbon, same thing. I was just another G.I. spending all my time and money in pubs and bars. Art was on hold!

I can't say that I didn't log any time sketching while I was over there, for I did take my sketch pad along with me to different countries, but all the sketch pads had the same subject matter, as if they belonged to Latrec or Vincent VanGogh because most of my subject matter was of the nightlife in the bars throughout Europe.

I would like to go into more detail of my flying experiences and memories of my travels throughout Europe and Africa, but that would take another book, and I'm trying to keep this book's contents down to my art as much as possible and how it relates to my life in later years. However, there are a couple of stories that relate to how I arrived at the point in my life I am today.

We were in Oslo, Norway, and our plane was overloaded with two jet engines on board. On take off we were going full power down the runway trying to gain enough air speed to lift off. Three-fourths of the way down the runway, past the point of "no return", our left engine started backfiring and smoking. Our pilot feathered that prop and gave full power to our remaining engine, About that time Oslo tower called me on the radio and stated. "A. F. 646, your left engine is smoking and backfiring on take off." There was a lot of panic going on in that cockpit and all I could reply back to the tower was, "No shit!"!

Now, the countryside around Oslo Airport was all pine trees and lakes, lakes and pine trees. We didn't have enough runway left by that time to abort, so it left the pilot no alternative but to try to get airborne on a single engine. The grove of pine trees at the end of the runway was coming up quicker than the one hundred twenty knots of airspeed that we needed for take off. With the coals poured to our remaining right engine, the pilot pulled back on the stick just in time to barely clear the tree tops at the end of the runway. We could literally hear the tops of the pine tree brushing the bottom of the fuselage as we cleared them.

All this time the pilot was trying to get the aircraft turned around in a wide sweep to return to Oslo Airport. This procedure went on over and over, losing altitude, clipping tree tops, but just gaining enough altitude to clear the next grove of trees. Finally, we landed and taxied up to the tower and got out of the aircraft. I stood there with my crew chief looking at out airplane, talking about our hair-raising experience with airport officials. I found myself trying to smoke a cigarette, but I was shaking so badly I couldn't hit my mouth with the cigarette. Now, the crew chief was a veteran of World War II and already had several close calls in his flying career, even having to bail out a couple of aircraft in his time. He saw I was trying to hit my mouth with the cigarette and told me that during the war he had been in the same situation. Then he advised me to take my silk scarf that the flight crew always wore, throw it over my neck, take one end and put it in my left hand then take the other end of the scarf with my cigarette in my right hand, then slowly pull the left hand holding the end of my scarf down. This brought the right hand with my cigarette up to my mouth. This way, no mater how much I was shaking I could hit my mouth. After we had talked to the Oslo Airport officials, the crew had to catch a flight back to out home base in Evereux, France.

It was mandatory that one of the crew stay with the disabled aircraft. Usually, it was an unmarried crew member, and beings I was the only single crew member, I was chosen to stay in Oslo with our aircraft. The rest of the crew went back to Evereux to get a new engine.

After a couple of days the engine was mounted and we were ready to take ole 646 back to our home base. It was late at night before we finally took off. About eleven P.M., as we were flying over the North Sea on our way home, we hit one of the worse thunderstorms that we ever flew through. Nowadays, aircraft fly over or around big thunderstorms, but back in those days you just had to buckle up and hit them straight on. Here it was, pitch black, midnight, flying over the North Sea and if you had to ditch your aircraft at sea, you had only a matter of seconds, not even enough time to get from your aircraft to a life raft before freezing to death. There were four kids in that cockpit, Pappy, out pilot was the ripe old age of twenty four.

Lightning was striking us upside down and backward. It was bouncing around the cargo compartment and coming into the cockpit. Lightning so bad that it blew the static discharges off our wings and tail.

Static discharges are like little rope looking things about ten inches long that take static electricity and lightning off the aircraft, but we were getting such a huge amount of lightning it blew them to smithereens.

Our aircraft was bouncing around like crazy and it was all pappy could do to keep the aircraft upright. During all that time static electricity, Saint Elmo's Fire, or Foxfire, a bright green glow was building up on our props, soon it was bouncing across the windshields and beings there was no static dischargers to get rid of it, it started building up all over the aircraft. It seemed to be three feet thick over the entire aircraft. It was bouncing all over the place; our aircraft was a solid green glow in the worse thunder storm imaginable.

Well, just about that time all hell broke loose. It was like a thousand light bulbs blew up in our faces, Some of our instruments blew out and we couldn't see. It seemed like a good twenty minutes. When we finally could see again, we were out of the storm. We all sat there in silence as we winged our way home in the dark of night.

After the hair-raising experience in Oslo as week and a half earlier, I'll tell you, we were sure scared. I'm glad I was just a dumb kid. You couldn't get me back in one of those C-119's today even on a bluebird day, much less in those kinds of conditions.

This story relates to how I came up with what I would finally name my farm; FoxFire Farm.

The other story of my flying career is about how I got out of the Air Force. It was when the U.S. was building a top secret base in Turkey, and we were flying in supplies and material to build this site. From Evereux we flew to Spain, then across to Casablanca. Those old aircraft didn't have very long range on their gas tanks so every few hundred miles we would stop and refuel to get us another couple hundred miles.

From Casablanca we flew to Tunis, Tunisia, then to Algiers, Algeria, and then to Tripoli, Libya, Athens, Greece, and then on into Turkey, making refueling stops all the way.

Well, during the mid '50's the Algerians and the French were in a full scale war. The base that we had to land in was French controlled, but in Algerian rebel territory. When coming in for a landing at the French base low level, we had to fly right over Algerian territory. The Algerians were imbedded at the end of the runway and would take pot shots at the aircraft as we were landing. Knowing this, we always carried bullet proof jackets when flying this route. We didn't have to worry about wearing the bullet proof jackets to protect us from aircraft fire; we only had to worry about ground fire as we were coming in on final approach, so we always sat on our bullet proof jackets because if you were going to "get it" that was were it was going to be.

This one particular landing at Algiers we were picking up the usual ground fire whizzing through the cargo compartment but we made a safe landing about dusk. The main gear had just touched down and as I was turning in my seat after getting taxi instructions from the tower, I had one hand on each side of my seatbelt and about that time we looked up and noticed the Algerians had snuck out on the French base and strung concrete blocks across the runway just in front of our aircraft. The pilot saw the concrete blocks just in time to lift the nose over, but our main gear hit them dead on. I froze when I noticed the blocks and didn't get my safty belt hooked together in time. Our aircraft spun around in the middle of the runway and I went through the instrument panel, screwing up my back.

I ended up spending a few days in an Algerian hospital. During my recuperation the Air Force put me up in this luxurious place called the Saint George Hotel. This was in the summer of 1956 and it was one of the most plush hotels I had ever seen.

I found out after I married my second wife, Charlie, that as a little girl she was also staying in that hotel at the same time I was. I probably saw her running around the halls or in the gardens. I teased Charlie later, "Do you remember an Air Force man saying to you, Little girl, want some candy?"

Well, that little mishap was the end of my flying days. When I got back to Evereux they took me off flight status. The Air Force was afraid if I ever had to bail out it would throw my back out of whack. I spent the last six months of my military career painting murals on the walls of the base chow halls in France.

I wanted to go to a chiropractor but the Air Force did not believe in chiropractors so they gave me an early out. That way, I could go to a chiropractor in civilian life.

**CIVILIAN LIFE**:

I was discharged from the Air Force early in 1957. There was a recession going on and you couldn't buy a job. I came back home to Carthage, but, of course, there was no such thing as an artist job in this area.

I bought a car with my money I had saved and drove all over the country looking for an art job: Boston, New Orleans, Los Angels, everywhere I applied for a job I was asked the same question. "Do you have experience in commercial art?" My pat answer was, "How am I supposed to get experience if I can't find a job?"

I finally came back t Carthage and decided to go to college. I went to two different colleges in the area. I took all the art courses first, thinking I would take the required courses later. After two years I had taken al the art courses and never did get around to taking Algebra, English, and the other required courses.

I finally landed a job working for a printing company, sweeping floors, cleaning presses, anything, hoping I would get to do any work that was needed, like letterheads or brochures that required some art work. Only about half my time was actually spent doing art, but that was OK, at least I was getting some experience. It seemed getting that first job was the foothold to get into the art world.

During the next year I worked at three or four different printing companies. At least I was gaining experience. The one day I decided to go into business for myself.

I rented a little building in Carthage, right next to the Boots Drive-In, the main hangout for the young people of the area. I mean, it was where all the chicks hung out! And there was my new studio overlooking the parking lot. I had a bird's nest on the ground. I painted a big sign with a fox in a beret holding a paint brush and I called my new business "Pierre's Commercial Art."

One day I was sitting in my studio looking out the window with a friend of mine, Mouse Morris, when a red and white '55 Buick buzzed Boots. (Buzzing Boots, it was called). There were three girls in the car and I turned to my friend and said, "Hey, Mouse, who is that girl driving the Buick?" He said her name was "Nancy something or other" and then said, "She's new in town. She moved here from Salem, Missoura, a couple of weeks ago."

I told Mouse, "I'm going to marry that girl" and from that day on I started bird-dogging her. I finally got to meet this Nancy chick and I turned all the charm on her that I could muster up and started dating her.

# Chapter 2

**Pierre's Studio in Carthage**

## MY PIERRE DAYS:

During the time I was dating Nancy, I was making ends meet by hustling companies in the area doing letterhead art and designing brochures for their businesses. I was doing okay. I even started getting commissions to do oil paintings for people and this was right up my alley.

That last year, before Nancy and I were married, I received a big commission from a new motel south of Carthage called the Rawhide Motel. They wanted nine big western paintings. I didn't know "come here from sic-um" about cowboys and Indians, so I had to fake it by copying paintings of Charles Russell and changing them around enough so that the paintings wouldn't appear to be a direct rip-off. Besides, I signed the paintings Pierre Davis. I wouldn't have dared put my name Lowell Davis on them. I was saving that name just in case I ever hit the big time.

I made enough money off those paintings that Nancy and I thought we could get married, which we did in April of 1959. I even had enough money left over to buy a little red sports car.

I was still working on commissions, but by now jobs were getting scarce as hen's teeth. I knew I was going to have to face up to the fact that I wasn't making it as a free lance artist. I was going to have to get a real job.

It was about that time that I ran into Nan Beck, a long time friend from the fifth grade. I told Nan about my situation and that I needed a company I could work for that would bring me a steady income. Nan told me she had an uncle that owned M.W.M. Color Press in Aurora. It was a huge company, especially for this area, with their staff including more than forty artist. I got the job, but I didn't enjoy the ninety miles commute each day.

I had worked for M.W.M. about a month and I wasn't happy with the type of art work I was doing. The company's main business was doing post cards and church bulletins. My job was taking a photograph of the church or business and air-brushing out power lines, cars, telephone poles, and the like. I told them the work they were putting out was hum-drum. "This is the '60's, and it's time for a change. We need to be creative and innovative," I told them. Of course, they told me to go sit down at my drawing board and keep air-brushing out those little telephone poles.

It was about a week later that a man from Texas walked into M.W.M. It was John Newburn – their biggest customer. Now, Mr. Newburn made frequent visits to M.W.M., coming up from Texas to check on his printing business. But this time he was in Aurora for more than his routine visit. He was on a mission. He was going to start an art department in his company, Nationwide Advertising, in the Dallas, Texas, area, and he wanted an artist from M.W.M. to head up the department.

Being as Mr. Newburn was their biggest client, he was told he could have his pick of the litter for his new art department. John Newburn spent the best part of the day going through the different artist's portfolios. He made his selection and when he told the owner of M.W.M. that he had chosen me, the owner said, "Oh no! You don't want him! He's a Beatnik. He has a sports car and….." then went on to tell him that I was always trying to make changes for the coming 1960's.

They tried their best to discourage him. John was such a good customer they didn't want to make him angry by siccing me on him, but the more they tried to discourage him by telling him all my bad traits, the more John Newburn wanted me. Finally, they gave in saying they had tried to talk him out of it, and he was not to hold M.W.M. responsible if I didn't work out!

Mr. Newburn was aware of the '60's revolution and it didn't bother him. He walked up to my drawing board and said, "Son, how would you and your new bride like to move to Texas and start up an art department in my company, National Advertising?" He went on to tell me of all the great features of the company. Also he would pay all my moving expenses. He offered me $100.00 dollars a week and said he was going to make an "executive" out of me.

That day, the day he offered me the job, was a very hot August day. M.W.M. was in an old building and its only air-conditioning was to just open the windows. I always had trouble keeping my sweat from dripping on my art work. That, in itself, was almost enough to make me say, "yes". Also I thought, "A hundred bucks a week. Wow!" That was all the money in the world to me since I was only making minimum wages at the time and that was only $1.25 an hour. And to be an executive to boot! I thought I had died and gone to Heaven. We shook hands and John Newburn peeled off a couple of hundred dollar bills and handed them to me for moving expenses. Then I was outta there!.

I went home to Carthage where Nancy and I were living with my parents. We threw all our belongings into the trunk of the little sports car and we were Texas bound!

**Nancy and Lowell Texas Bound**

When I arrived at Nationwide Advertising Company, it was even better than I expected. I was given a big, brand new office with a big picture window that overlooked the parking lot. John Newburn also gave me a carte blanch art supply expense account.

Off I went to the art supply shop. I was like a kid in a candy shop. I spent more money on art supplies that day then I ever dreamed possible.

Always before, Nationwide farmed out all their art needs. Now, John wanted me to hire three or four more artists, which I did. The bulk of the work we did was designing brochures, catalogs, and direct mail pamphlets. I loved my new job, but I still had this burning desire to be a cartoonist. Every chance I got, I worked at home drawing cartoons and sending them out to different magazines. This met with only minor success, but at least it did pay the rent.

In August of 1961, about a year after moving to Texas, Nancy and I had our first baby, a little girl we named April. From that day to this, April is still my little girl and the joy of my life.

The next couple of years things plugged along the same at Nationwide with me drawing and designing brochures, and that type of art. Then one day John came into my office and said, "Pierre, I know how much you like doing cartoons and I have a great idea." He wanted to put out a little risqué cartoon book. Businesses around the country could buy it and put their ad on the back of it and give them to their customers as a gift. This was called an advertising specialty item. The he said, "Pierre, I want you to draw all the cartoons for the new book and I'll let the other artists that work here take over your duties."

I was going to finally do what I had always wanted to do since I was a little kid, be a full-time cartoonist.

The cartoon book was more than a success. It was a hit! John then wanted me to do more books, so , I drew about six more. Next, he decided to take all the advertising specialty booklets and combine them into one big cartoon magazine. It would be sold on the newsstands instead of businesses using them for their advertisements. John Newburn then gave birth to the tenth best-selling magazine in America, for a reason. I haven't figured out to this day why John named the magazine *"Sex to Sexty"*.

It was now in the mid '60's and the Vietnam War was in full swing. The flower children and the Hippies were out in all their glory. I had to hire three more full time cartoonists to put out the now monthly publication. Half of our shipments of *"Sex to Sexty"* were going to our servicemen in Vietnam.

It was 1965; the year God gave Nancy and me one of His greatest rewards, a son. We named him Phillip.

By this time I was growing weary of fulfilling my dream of being a cartoonist, decided I wanted to be a wildlife artist, but, in those days there was no such thing as wildlife paintings in any gallery in the United States that I knew of. The only way at that time to paint wildlife and sell it commercially, was to put the paintings on magazine covers and wildlife calendars. So instead of me working all night sending out cartoons to different magazines, I decided to paint wildlife. That's when I first started using the name Lowell Davis.

I began sending out transparencies of my wildlife paintings to magazines like *Spots a Field, Outdoor Life, Fur, Fish and Game*, and others, hoping to get one of my paintings on their covers. Although I sold a few paintings for magazine covers, it wasn't enough so I could quit my job at Nationwide.

About this time, I was hearing more and more about an artist in Arlington. Joe Grandee, who painted western art. I had been watching Joe's growth and success and Nancy and I talked about this success frequently. Joe had an agent at the time. A Dr. Rainone, a very influential dentist in the Dallas-Fort Worth area.

One day Nancy picked up a bunch of my original paintings I had meant to be covers for wildlife magazines and drove to Dr. Rainone's home. She walked up and rang the doorbell and when he answered, told him she was my wife and could he possibly sell my original wildlife paintings?

At that time Dr. Rainone's thoughts were the same as mine. He had never seen wildlife paintings for sale in any gallery in the area, but he told Nancy he would hold onto a few of the paintings to see if he could get any response from the collectors he came into contact with while handling Joe Grandee's work.

Nancy left five original wildlife paintings with Dr. Rainone and that very weekend he called me on the phone and said, "Lowell, I don't know what happened, but a couple of gallery owners from west Texas came by my house and I showed them your wildlife paintings. One of the gallery owners bought three and the other guy bought the other two." He then said, "I think it was a fluke, but if you have anymore originals would you have your wife bring them to my house?" So, Nancy gathered up several more originals I had laying around the house and took them over to Dr. Rainone. A few days later Dr. Rainone calls again, "Guess what Lowell? I had a couple of gallery owners come in and they bought all your paintings. They want to sign a contract with you and buy at least three of your paintings a month."

Dr. Rainone was aware I wasn't very interested in being a full time cartoonist. He knew I longed to be a wildlife artist, and he felt comfortable with the enthusiasm from the gallery owners. He also thought it was the right time for me to quit the advertising agency.

By this time the magazine *"Sex to Sexty"* was going great and John Newburn had enough free lance cartoonists to keep the monthly publication going, but he did love my cover paintings so he asked me for one favor, and that was to continue doing the covers for *"Sex to Sexty"*. at least one a month. I told him I would gladly do that, but after six years at Nationwide, I felt I was ready to get on with my career adventure.

Now, I was also getting serious about sculpting and got heavily involved doing wildlife bronzes. I was doing quite well with the bronzes, but I did have one big problem, after all this living in the Dallas area, I was sick of it and hated everything about living in the big city.

It continued to eat at me night and day. I found out it was easy to get locked into big cities and harder than hell to get out of them. In the early '60's I was for and into change, but by the mid '60's I hated all the changes that were going on around me and I wanted out. I wanted to get back to basics. I hated our big city lifestyle, but my wife Nancy loved it and was not willing to move.

So, I buried myself in my work, mostly painting wildlife and doing bronze sculptures. I was still doing my one-a-month painting for *"Sex to Sexty."* I painted a total of 250 covers in eighteen years I worked for that magazine. All of the originals are still hanging in the halls and offices of Nationwide Advertising in Arlington, Texas.

In 1969 Nancy gave birth to the cutest little girl you ever laid eyes on and we named her Heather.

Now, we had three beautiful children. Nancy was a very pretty lady and I thought she was the reason that I was throwing such good looking kids, but later on in my life, after I was married to Charlie, we had two more beautiful babies. That's when I realized it must be me throwing those handsome children. I thought other women would see all my good looking offspring and would want to hire me out for stud service, but believe it or not, to this day, I haven't received one damn phone call.

During the time I sold my art through Dr. Rainone, he would ask me what I wanted out of my art. My reply was always the same, "I want out of this rat race. I want to get a farm somewhere." I enjoyed working with Dr. Rainone, he was a great man with a wonderful family and I didn't mind paying his twenty five percent commission on the art work he sold as my exclusive agent, but all that changed the day a gallery owner from west Texas called and said Kaiser Porcelain factory in Germany was looking for an American wildlife sculptor. The company that was distributing Kaiser Porcelain figurines in the U.S. was Ebbling & Russ out of Philadelphia. They had about thirty sales people on the road and Kaiser had asked them to keep an eye out for a good American wildlife sculptor.

Kaiser had tried using their German sculptors to sculpt our wildlife but they just weren't pulling it off. The sculptors had to use zoo animals or encyclopedias for reference materials, and while American hunters were willing to pay the price for wildlife sculptures, they weren't buying the German interpretation.

One of the Ebbling & Russ salesman walked into the gallery in west Texas saw my wildlife bronzes, and said to the gallery owner, "That's the American artist I think Kaiser is looking for," and with that the owner of the gallery called me and told me the story.

Later on, that same week, Ebbling & Russ contacted me and we agreed to meet in Philadelphia to sign a contract. As I said earlier, I didn't mind paying the twenty five percent agent's fee for individual paintings and sculptures, but when I signed with Ebbling & Russ I was still supposed to pay Dr. Rainone the twenty five percent commission everything I sold, just because he was my exclusive agent? The only thing he had to do with getting my contract was selling a gallery the wildlife bronzes that the Ebbling & Russ representative had seen.

It began eating on me constantly. I just couldn't believe Dr. Rainone was going to get twenty five percent of everything I was going to make from now on. Dr. Rainone and I started with a handshake agreement and now, I've never broken a deal or my word with any man, much less a handshake, but I just couldn't stand the thought. So, I just disappeared out of sight and never again had contact with Dr. Rainone.

I felt so bad; I never used any of Dr. Rainone's contacts or contacted any galleries where he had placed any of my work. I owe a great gratitude to Dr. Rainone for he is the man that taught me that my originals would sell. He also taught me how to tell a good painting from a bad one. I never sold any paintings to anyone that could in any way have been influenced by Dr. Rainone.

I started going to art shows outside the state of Texas. Everything was going well in sales and I was having sell out shows all across the country. Kaiser was selling well too, so I guess you could say I was rich! Really rich for the first time in my life. I built a big beautiful log and stone home for Nancy outside of Arlington, near Lake Arlington, but I still wasn't happy. All I could think about was getting out of the big city.

I guess that's what caused Nancy to finally get a divorce. She was tired of hearing me complain about Texas, so one day I came home from a show in Las Vegas and upon my arrival, instead of coming home to my wife's open arms, It was just a finger and that finger was pointing "Out, Get out!"

Now, I wanted out of Texas, but this wasn't exactly what I had in mind. When I drove north out of Texas I was one hurting puppy. All that drive I had to pull off the side of the highway to puke and cry. When I crossed that Texas state line I left Pierre behind.

I drove back to Carthage and moved in with my parents. Six months after Nancy and I were separated, I still wasn't dealing with my situation any better. I still woke up in the morning, the nights that I could sleep, I was drenched with sweat. I still hadn't talked to anyone to speak of in six months, not even my parents. My insides were so twisted that I was gagging and vomiting all day and night.

I tried painting every day to get my mind off feeling sorry for myself. My paintings were awful. It seemed like I was taking my hurt out on the canvas. My paintings were ugly, dark, muddy and grim. Picasso had his blue period of painting. I called this my grey period.

Then, one day I got a phone call from an old sales rep of Ebbling & Russ, distributor of my Kaiser Figurine line. I had been working for them at the time of my divorce but in anger and hurt, I had told Kaiser and Ebbling & Russ earlier to shove the contract as I didn't want to work for them, but I didn't want to work for anyone anymore.

The sales representative, Jerry Cooper, who called me said he had heard rumors of my problem. He said, "Lowell, I heard of the slump you are going through and I think you need a change of pace. Gather up your paintings and come down to the Gift Mart in Atlanta." He went on to say, "Lowell, you have just gotta get yourself out of your slump. I'll set you up in the corner of our showroom. You need to talk to your collectors and I know I can sell some of your originals."

Well, reluctantly, I bundled up my Grey Period paintings and flew to Atlanta. I was planning on being there for all five days of the show. I tried talking to the people who approached me and my paintings and showed some interest, but my tongue was thick and I just kinda drooled when I tried to talk to them. I was sweating all the poison and pity out of my system all day and night, and it didn't matter how many showers I took, I smelled like a goat.

After the third day, Jerry, who had been observing me talking and trying to react positively to people finally came over to me and said, "Hey, Lowell, I'm sorry, but you are not doing us any good here in the showroom and we aren't doing you any good. So, maybe it's best if you pack up and go back to your parent's house." He also suggested I might want to stay in the cabin that he had in the mountains of north Georgia. There was a stream running through by the back door and I was welcome to go there and sit and stare and maybe that would help. I thanked him anyway for all his efforts to bring me out of my depression.

I left Gift Mart then my depression went into full swing. I caught a cab and headed for the bars in the Atlanta slum area. I figured that was going to be my new home from now on. So I spent the next two days and nights in that ghetto. Up to this point, since my divorce, I really hadn't had a drink to speak of.

The main reason I hadn't been able to drown my troubles was that my mama didn't allow drinking in her house. Secondly, I wasn't about to go outside and meet anyone, or go to a bar, because I didn't want to run into someone I knew.

When the cab let me off, the first thing I did was find a country bar where I decided to get blitzed, and stay blitzed making the streets my permanent residence.

I had sold a couple of paintings at the show and had a pocket full of money, which I used to buy drinks for the house. I sure did make a lot of good wino friends that way. We drank together and I listened to their stories. To this point I still wasn't talking to anyone, just listening to their stories of how we ended up together.

Never before had I liked or listened to country music, but now I kept shoving money into the jukebox, from breakfast to midnight. It was then that all those country songs started making sense. They really started hitting home, and it seemed like they were all written for me.

After the third day I found myself waking up with the biggest head you can imagine. IN fact, it was so heavy I could hardly lift my head from the sidewalk. I finally managed to slither over to a door and prop myself up against it. I fumbled through my pockets and found my trusty corn cob pipe, lit it and tried to ignore my throbbing head. It was July, 1973, and Georgia sun was just coming up.

I looked around and saw some of my new found friends sleeping in a doorway, one of them even managed to find a bench. As I sat there, pondering my new environment and said to myself, "Hey, Lowell! Are you really enjoying this as much as you thought?" As I looked around my fallen comrades I got to thinking about the sob stories they had told me over the last two days. I thought, y'know, these men weren't always winos and drunkards living on the streets. They were bankers, accountants, a dentist, fathers, and husbands. They had homes at one time. All of them were men who had come to a crisis in their lives and just couldn't cope. After I had finished smoking my pipe for the third time and all the time thinking, "Is this really the lifestyle I want?" of course the answer was "No!"

I managed to get myself in an upright position and checked my pockets to see if I have enough money for a cab to the airport. It was sure a good thing I had purchased a round trip ticket from Joplin to Atlanta, because I barely had enough to pay for the cab, much less buy an airline ticket back to Joplin.

When I got to the airport I went into the men's room, got some paper towels, and gave myself a whore's bath as best as I could, and then headed out to my gate. Threw down some aspirins I had picked up at a news counter and prayed they would start immediate effect.

The announcement came over the loud speaker for the loading of the St. Louis passengers. Then, luckily, I remembered I was one of them. Usually, I entertain myself at airports by people-watching, but today I was oblivious of anyone being around me. I made my way through the gate and through the aircraft aisle to my seat assignment. I finally managed to find it. It was an aisle seat and there was no one sitting in the window or center seats. I thought to myself, "Oh, how could I be so lucky to have all three seats to myself so I can lie down." Also, this particular morning I really needed to lie down. Those seats looked so soft after sleeping on the sidewalk for two nights.

## Chapter 3

**Charlie and Lowell on the bank of the Arkansas River**

CHARLIE:

The plane was still loading a few late passengers, so I decided to slump down in my seat, pull the hat down over my eyes and hope those aspirins would start doing their thing. Not lifting the bill of my hat, I felt all the passengers had taken their seats and I was getting ready to flop over into the two vacant seats when a young lady tapped me on the knee. when I looked up, she motioned she was sitting in my window seat.

Just as she was seated and buckled up, a man stood in the aisle by my seat and motioned that I move my knees so he could sit in the center seat between me and the girl by the window.

I overheard him talking to her although not picking up on any of their conversation. I just assumed they were together. I pulled my hat down over my eyes again and then realized if I was going to snooze, it was going to have to be sitting up.

We taxied out to the runway and took off. As soon as we got airborne the smoking light came on, I needed sleep, but I also needed to fire up my old pipe at the same time. So, the pipe won out. I shuffled through my pockets for my lighter and couldn't find it. I then thought it must be in my jacket in the overhead. I stood up and started fumbling through the overhead compartment looking for my lighter, when the girl next to the window said, "Need a match?"

She handed me a book of matches, smiled, and said, "Keep them." As I thanked her I studied her face for the first time and thought, "Gosh! I wish that man wasn't with her."

As I sat there smoking my pipe and drinking a cup of coffee which the stewardess said I looked like I needed, my headache was dissipating. As soon as we reached cruising altitude, the man in the middle seat unfastened his seat belt and excused himself, stood up, and went into the aisle to go to the restroom. Shortly after he headed aft, the girl by the window tapped me on the shoulder and asked, "Excuse me, but would you sit in the seat next to me or call the stewardess? This man has been following me all through the airport, trying to talk to me. He's supposed to be in the non-smoking section."

I said, "Sure, I'll sit by you." It wasn't long before, for the first six months, I found myself so in tune with this girl I couldn't stop talking. We talked for the entire two hour flight from Atlanta to St. Louis. It was like I had diarrhea of the mouth. She couldn't get a word in edgewise. She did get to say she was from Tulsa and that she just came out og South Carolina where she had attended a college girlfriend's wedding.

When we arrived at the Louis Airport and checked our flight schedules, hers was going to Tulsa and mine was going to Joplin. We noticed we both had about an hour and a half layover. I asked if she was like to have a drink with me, kind of a hair of th e dog sort of drink for me. She accepted, and we found ourselves sitting in the airport lounge, talking again. The bartender asked for her identification and when she showed it to him and he brought her a glass of wine, I was sure relieved. At least she was twenty one! Somewhere in our conversation, unlike in the TWA flight to St. Louis, I allowed her to talk.

She told me she went a year to Mills College, in Oakland, then her second year she went to the University of Southern France. Beings she was raised in France and North Africa, she spoke fluent French. We talked a lot about Europe, Africa and France, and since we both spent a lot of time in those countries, we reminisced together. Then, she told me she went to her junior year of college to Oral Roberts University in Tulsa, but didn't think she was going back there in the fall. There were too many restrictions, especially after spending a year on her own at the University of Southern France in Marseilles.

Now, she was working through the summer at City Service Petroleum in Tulsa, where her father was the chief operations geophysicist. Then, I told her I bought art supplies in Tulsa and the next time I came to Tulsa I would giver her a ring to see if she would consider going out to dinner some night with an old man. She said, "I don't know! Try me!"

Her name was Charlie. She gave me her phone number and we said our goodbyes.

About a week later, back at my parent's house in Carthage, I realized I was getting low on some art supplies, so I called and arranged a date with Charlie. After that date, I was realizing I was needing art supplies about every week. After about four weekends in a row I decided I'd save a lot on gas if I moved to Tulsa.

By that time I was coming out of my recluse period. I was beginnin' to feel a little bit better about life and there would be small breaks in my days that I wasn't feeling sorry for myself.

Charlie was young, she was fun, and I really enjoyed her company. She was the only girl I dated since my divorce. In fact, she was the only girl I had dated since I met Nancy some fourteen years earlier.

I got a small room in Tulsa where the bed pulled down from out of the wall and had enough room so I could put up an easel and paint during the day. Most nights Charlie and I would have a date. After our date I would take Charlie home to her parent's house and go back to my lonely little apartment, pull the bed out of the wall, and lie there and stare at those four little walls.

I enjoyed being with Charlie because it took my mind off my feeling sorry for myself, but then, laying there in that bed, it would all come back to me: thirteen years of working night and day, my beautiful home, our three cars, the big art collection, furniture, my wife and kids-all gone. The only thing I had left with from the marriage was what was in my studio that I was able to load in my car, and I even ended up with the car that still had payments. I would lay in there in bed and think about it, over an over, and cry myself to sleep.

To this day I will see Nancy and say, "Nancy, what happened to cause us to get a divorce? What was the reason?" And to this day when I ask her that question her eyes just cloud up and she says, "I don't know", and walks away.

Oh, I did drive back to Texas to pick up my motorcycle.

Charlie's parents had a big beautiful house in an exclusive area overlooking Tulsa. Her parents always greeted me at the door with a welcome smile. A lot of nights they would fix dinner for us before we went out. Some night we just stayed at their house and after dinner, her father Joe, and I would play dominos. Then, one summer night I had rode my motorcycle over to their house to pick her up, and later after a movie we stopped on the banks of the Arkansas River. As we watched the moon glistening on the water I turned to Charlie and said, "Charlie, there is something in your home that your parents have. If I would have had it in my home in Texas, I wouldn't have been going through what I've been through the last eight months."

She turned to me and said, "Well, that's easy. It's Jesus Christ."

I said, "Bullshit!"

"Well, you asked," she said. "It's Jesus Christ!" I sat there and thought about it for awhile and the we got off on another subject.

That night after I took her home, and went back to that lonely little apartment, instead of crying myself to sleep, I just lay there and though about Charlie's answer. "Could that be true?" I knew I had never asked Christ to be part of my life. Now, when I was growing up my parents had me in church every Sunday morning, Sunday evenings and sometimes Wednesdays, and all tent revivals. They were Pentecostal. When I joined the Air Force, I said to myself, "I ain't never goin' to another church", and for the past eighteen years I had done a damn good job of keeping that vow to myself.

Oh, I believe in God alright, and I prayed if smoke was filling up the cockpit while I was flying with the Air Force, or when we lost an engine in those old airplanes I prayed quite often, and I prayed when one of my babies was really sick. But other than that, that was about all the religion I had in me.

I don't think I slept much that night thinking about could that be it? All the time I was living in Texas, I was the ultimate liberal; meaning I depended on the government or my own self for all my needs, instead of God. I thought I had everything under control: Wrong! I came home and was kicked out. I lost everything in one night. Even over the next two or three months I kept thinkin' about it. I would go back over to her parent's house and I would sit there and try to get the feeling if what she told me was true.

I knew Charlie had lived in Algiers, North Africa, and was raised in a big villa with maids and chauffeurs and every time I went to pick her up, I expected her dad to meet me at the door, step outside and say to me, "Look, Lowell, you are fifteen years older than our daughter. You've been married, have three children, and you are divorced. We raised our daughter in the finest girl's schools, and we raised her very proper. You are not exactly what we had in mind for her. So, maybe you should go jump back on your motorcycle and head off into the sunset and don't come back anymore." But he never did. Her parents always welcomed me and made me feel welcome in their home that had a warm glow inside.

October, 1973, came and I received a phone call. A phone call I had wanted to receive for eight months. It was Nancy! She called to see if we might be able to give our marriage another try. I went over to Charlie's home that night and on that date I told her I was moving back to Texas the next day.

Charlie was devastated. She had hoped we had more of a future together than that!

I went back to my kids and Nancy and up through Christmas of '73 we faked at getting our love back together, but by New Year's Day, we realized it wasn't going to work. I packed my measly belongings into my car and had Texas in my rear view mirror for the last time.

I headed back to Tulsa in hopes that I could get back with Charlie, but when I got their and tried to call her house, the number had been changed. They had an unlisted number. So, I drove over to the house. This time her dad did meet me at the door and said Charlie had gone out for the evening and that after I had hurt her so much by getting her hopes up and falling in love with me, and then me leaving, it would be best if I hadn't come back. Although he had great respect for me for going back to Texas and trying to get my marriage back together, he said it would still be best if I didn't try to contact Charlie.

By this time I had fallen deeply in love with Charlie and I knew what he was talking about. I went back to my little apartment and lay there thinking of how I was still screwing up my life and that I desperately needed some relief.

A couple of days later, I was still thinking about Jesus Christ, as the answer, so the next days I called Joe at his office and asked if there was anyway possible he and Jean, Charlie's mother, could come over to my apartment that evening. He said they would.

When they arrived that evening, I shared with them for the first time, how I had made a muck of my life and I was tired of trying to run my own life, and that from now on I wanted to turn my life over to the Lord and let Him lead me and take over my future. They were certainly glad to pray with me. The three of us got on our knees around the coffee table, held hands and prayed to get rid of my sins and to accept Christ into my life. It was a tearful but joyful night. Still, as they were leaving, they said, "Lowell, we are so glad you have accepted Christ into your life this evening, but it doesn't change the way we feel about you seeing Charlie again."

I agreed not to try to make contact with her. They left and I packed up and moved back home to Carthage and lived with my parents.

Although I felt a great joy in my life and I was painting good again, I was still missing the hell out of Charlie. It seemed like months since that night, but it must have been about a fortnight when the phone rang at my parent's house. It was Charlie! She and her parents were driving back from Mexico, listening to the radio, and they heard I was having a show at Utica Square in Tulsa. She also told me she had been dating two or three guys but they just couldn't replace me.

I said, "Well, hell, I could have told you that!"

After that phone call, we met secretly for a few weekends. I would drive to Tulsa and we would meet at the Denny's restaurant, our favorite place to sit and talk, and where we always seemed to end up when we were dating.

After a few dates she told her parents we were still in love. Reluctantly they realized they weren't going to be able to keep us apart, so they once again welcomed me into their home.

I moved back to Tulsa and rented a cute little house, built during the 1920's in the Utica Square area. Now I was back to painting in full swing. I was even getting a lot of sculpting done and making a lot of wildlife bronze figurines.

While we were dating we talked about getting married and buying a farm. In April we decided to go to Oklahoma City and have Charlie's grandfather marry us. Charlie's mother said she was glad we were getting married, that way she might be able to get a good night's sleep.

Now, Joe, on the other hand, wasn't so receptive to the idea of our marriage. It was one thing for me to be dating his daughter, but marrying her was quite another. He said he was goin' on a business trip the day we planned to get married in Oklahoma City and wouldn't be in town. Although Joe liked me, he just didn't think out marriage would work out, especially since Charlie would be an instant mother to my three kids.

Charlie's relatives living in the Oklahoma City area attended our wedding along with her preacher grandfather, but her mom, Jean, didn't make it. She just stayed home and cried all day.

That night, after the wedding, I took her out to dinner at Long John Silver's and then we got a hotel room. I woke up the next morning at 4 A.M., slapped her on the ass and said, "Come on honey, get up. Let's go. I gotta get back to Tulsa and get to work." And work I did! My paint brushes were smokin' because we were flat broke.

No, I take that back. I had $750.00 dollars and Charlie had saved up $1000.00 dollars in her bank account. So, you see folks, I married Charlie for her money.

I had an art show in San Angelo, Texas and I needed to get some paintings ready for it. The show was going to be at Hemphill Wells, a chain of fine department stores throughout west Texas. I couldn't wait to impress my new bride at one of my shows with all the people standing in line to get my autograph. Well, when we arrived at Hemphill Well Department Store for the two day show, we found out they had advertised in newspapers, radio and television. They has been carrying my Kaiser Porcelain figurines for sometime in their gifts department, so that's where they put me. In the gift department with my figurines and the paintings. Charlie and I sat there in the gift department for two days and only one little ole lady came up to talk to me and she was asking directions to the lingerie department.

Boy, driving home all the way through west Texas after that show, I sure had my tail tucked between my legs. I really impressed my new bride!

People, to this day, when I am at a show and have a long line of people waiting to get my signature, say to me, "Lowell, don't you ever get tired of signing your name?" It happens most frequently at big shows like South Bend, Indiana, and Los Angeles, where we have the big gift show conventions and I sign my name for six straight hours I look at at them and say, "I would rather soak my hand in hot water in my hotel room at night than go through another Hemphill Well experience. It's much better for your arm to fall off from signing all day, than no one wanting your signature at all."

Our honeymoon a few weeks later consisted of borrowing my dad's pickup with a camper on the back, and heading for the northwest, Washington and Oregon, to about five shows and agent had set up for me. During that time I told Charlie I had always wanted to get a farm somewhere. So when we weren't driving or having shows, I kept looking with real estate folks for that perfect little farm. The farm I had been staring out the window of that advertising agency for so many years. As many places as we looked at, it just wasn't the right farm.

We came back to Tulsa, and on weekends we traveled the four-state area looking for it. Arkansas one weekend, nothing, Oklahoma another weekend, nothing, Kansas, the same thing.

All I knew is that it wasn't in Texas.

One weekend we drove to Carthage to stay with my parents and on the way into town I noticed a farm for sale on Highway 71, south of Carthage. The real estate name was Barney Scott Realty. I had never thought to look around the Carthage area where I grew up. Maybe it was because Nancy would have never allowed us to move to Carthage after living in Dallas. I said to Charlie, "Let's get up in the morning and call Scott Real Estate and go look at that farm."

So, the next morning that's what we did. Barney Scott first took us to the farm we passed coming into town. When we drove up to that that farm I said, "No, this is not it!" I asked if he had any other farms with small acreage. He took us to two more, same thing, and I said, "No, that's not it." He said, "That's it." I said, "You mean you don't have any more ideas or property to show us?"

Then he said, "Okay. I have one more little farm, but it's in real bad shape. No one has lived in it for several years." Barney had bought eighty acres and cut the 5-acre farm out of it and that was all he was willing to sell. I said, "Let's go look at it." We drove up Road 12, two miles east of Carthage, turned down a dirt road and I said, "That's it!" We were still a quarter mile away when I first saw it and even at that distance I knew this was it! The farm that I had dreamed about all those years in Texas.

As we drove closer my heart started pounding outta my chest. I was trying to play it cool with the real estate man there and all, but I was afraid in my excitement I was going to give my hand away. We drove into the driveway, through to the barn lot, parked and got out. Well, he was right! It was fallin' down alright. Weeds over my head, porches fallin' off, windows out of the house, barn and out buildings roofs caved in. But to me, it was the most beautiful farm I'd ever seen.

Just as I had imagined all those years, even down to the old privy in the orchard. As we were walking around the farm, I shoved my hands in my pockets trying to act as cool as I could. It wasn't until we got into the orchard and a covey of quail burst out of the weeds under my feet that in my excitement, I hollered, "I'll bye it!"

There was only one problem. I didn't have the $18,000.00 dollars he wanted for it. I didn't even have the $6,000.00 dollars it would take for the down payment. But never mind, I was going to raise that down payment some way!

Barney then told me the property lay adjacent to his farm and the only way he would sell it to me was if I promised to fix it up.

I promised!

To this day, when Barney comes over, I will ask him, "Well, Barney, did I fix her up enough to suit ya?"

## Chapter 4

**Foxfire Farm the day Charlie and Lowell bought the farm**

**THE FARM**:

After we shook hands on the farm deal with Barney, Charlie and I drove straight back to Tulsa. I'd just remembered a wealthy man in Fort Worth, who had told me a couple of years earlier that he would be interested in buying an original sculpture from me, if he could have it cast in bronze and sell the edition of thirty out for himself. So, that's what I was going to do, as soon as we got back to home.

When we hit the front door I sat down at my sculpting table and started sculpting. I was going to do a pair of fighting elk. I worked from sun up until late each night, without much more than a break for lunch, when Charlie would bring coffee and food to me.

In a record two and a half weeks I had finished the Fighting Elk sculpture. I put it in the back seat of the car and headed for Fort Worth. I handed that sculpture over to the man and he wrote me a check, for guess how much? $6,000.00 dollars!

I drove back to Tulsa, picked up Charlie and drove to Carthage. We walked in to Barney's real estate office and I plunked down the money, and we became the proud owners of my dream farm. But, even with the large down payment, the bank needed the house painted, the front porch roof fixed, and the windows put in before they would give us the balance of the loan.

It was September, 1974, Charlie and I packed out meager belongings and moved in with my parents. We worked on the necessary things that needed to be done on the farm so we could secure our loan from the bank.

Now, the closest Charlie had ever been to a farm was passing by one while driving down the highway. When we were dating I would be talking and showing her farms along the highway telling her how much I'd like to buy a farm and fix it up. Beings Charlie was raised in big cities, Europe, North Africa and South America, she would ask me, "What's it like living an a farm?" My answer was, "Well, on summer nights you can lie in your upstairs bedroom and let the south breeze blow across your body. Listen to bull frogs on the pond and hear coon hounds bayin' somewhere in the still of the night. A couple of years after that, I had a pond dug outside the bedroom window of the old farmhouse and stocked it with bull frogs. Then I bought her a blue tick hound pup and we named her Ozark Belle, to fulfill that statement that I made to her when we were dating.

When Charlie and I first bought the farm, she didn't know a combine from a plow, but she was sure eager to learn. The first thing we were required to do was have the house painted, so I hired this old time painter, Trent Poindexter. The first morning Trent came to work for us, he used some ole idiomatic expression, I can't remember what it was, but when we were out of his presence Charlie asked me what it meant. I realized then she has never been around country folks, and because she spoke fluent French and was raised with only proper English, she's never heard all the old clichés or idiomatic expressions. On the other hand, I had cut my teeth with country folks that used those kinds of phrases at every opportunity, so they didn't sound unusual to me.

The next day Charlie went to town and bought a little booklet. She started jotting down every idiomatic expression and cliché that she heard, along with any old home remedies she heard. For the past 25 years I have referred to her booklet anytime I needed to come up with a title for one of my figurines or paintings.

Adapt to farm life, Charlie did! I remember how hot it was that September, we were out in the Garden area pulling weeds together. I looked over at her with sweat dripping off her, mud streaks running down her face, he hands caked with dirt, and I thought to myself, "Now I got me a real woman here." My ex-wife Nancy's idea of roughing it was black and white television.

The first building I fixed up was the old fallen down chicken house. All my life I'd had chickens, mostly bantams. I've always loved chickens. The only time I didn't have chickens was when I was in the Air Force and those thirteen miserable years in the Dallas area. When I bought this farm I never wanted to be awakened again by an alarm clock, so the first farm critters I bought was fifteen chickens and eleven guineas. The next thing a farm needed was a dog. So, a couple of days after we got the farm we went out to the dog pound to find us a farm dog.

I said the the attendant at the pound, "I want the ugliest pup you have. A dog that nobody else would want. One so ugly you will put it to sleep." The attendant didn't disappoint me, He went back in the pens and brought me out this little female pup. All her hair was fallin' out from having mange and she was covered with blisters. The attendant said, "We are going to destroy this one this afternoon." I said, "That's the one I want."

So, I paid the man a dollar for that little dog, took her home, and nursed her back to health. We named her Hooker. That dollar dog later became my #1 model. She was to become the dog that paid for our farm. Over the years I've used her on fourteen limited edition plates, and about the same number of figurines. In fact, the very first figurine in my new farm series was Hooker by the mail box. It was titled "Country Road" and that was the piece that launched my whole farm figurine career.

Hooker used to go on all my touring engagements and was loved by all my collectors. When she died at the age of fourteen, I carved out a tombstone and buried her by the path leading from my house to the studio. The reason I sign the dog paw print on all my paintings, and every time I sign my name, is to pay tribute to Hooker.

Meanwhile, back on the ranch; Charlie and I finally got the house painted, the roof fixed and the front porch put back on. Then we fixed up three of the rooms to get the house livable, the kitchen, the bedroom, and an indoor bathroom. Charlie didn't mind roughin' it, but she drew the line when it came to using the outside privy in the orchard.

I'll never forget the first time Charlie's parents drove down to see our farm. They parked their Lincoln out in the barn lot, looked around at all the fallin' down buildings, weeds still over their heads, then came into the house that we were so proud of. It was all gutted out except for the three rooms and Joe and Jean turned to Charlie and said, "Come on honey, get your suitcase and we will get you outta here and take you home."

Even after we got the farm fixed up and they came to visit, they always walked around like they were afraid there were going to step in something.

By the time we got those three rooms and chicken house fixed up, we were dead broke again. All this time we had been working hard fixing up the house and I had also been working hard in my studio.

The studio was in the bedroom and I was painting wildlife and producing wildlife sculptures and having them cast in bronze. I had sold my motorcycle and my car and invested the money in the farm. Now I needed to start hitting some art shows and start selling again. But, we were carless, other than for an ole beat up '50 Ford pickup that we used to go to town and back and haul building supplies. I wouldn't have dared drive it any further thank I wanted to walk home.

Charlie's dad gave us an old Dodge car that he wanted to get rid of and my dad gave us his old tent trailer. Well, we put the two together, loaded up Hooker, paintings and bronzes, and headed off for the great Northwest. We also took along a lot of old wildlife prints I had left over from my career in Texas. We used the prints to barter for motel rooms and traded them to restaurants. That seemed to work well for restaurants and motels, but we didn't have any luck with gas station attendants.

That fall I had set up four or five weekend shows throughout the states of Washington and Oregon. We camped out in parks and camp sites and during the week I would paint and sculpt. During the weekend we would drive to cities like Spokane, Portland, Seattle and the tri-city area in Washington.

Then we headed back to Missoura, and our farm, with enough money to fix up another existing building.

Every time we finished fixing one up, we would go buy the animals that that particular building was supposed to house. Like when we fixed up the hog house, I would go buy a couple of pigs. When the goat house was done I bought four or five goats and so on.

The winter of 1974 was the worst winter I have ever experienced in Missoura. We had snow more than I could ever remember. For two weeks the ole thermometer hovered from 10 to 15 degrees below zero.

The pump in the well would freeze up several times a day. I would have to bundle up and head for the windmill, climb down in the dark damp hole under the windmill, and using my lighter, thaw out the switches. By the time I got back in the house my moustache and eyebrows were frosted or frozen, I remember it was so cold it couldn't snow except for this really fine snow.

The wind seemed to blow constantly those entire two weeks, and that fine snow would be in two little piles about two inches tall under each electrical receptacle in the kitchen. Those little piles of snow lasted for days, and yet the kitchen was the warmest room in the house.

We walked around the house wrapped in electric blankets and we didn't go any further than our cords would reach.

That winter, Charlie's and my marriage wasn't that secure. Her being a new bride and me so set in my ways, so she kept her suitcase packed and setting by the back door at all times, and about every two weeks she would grab her suitcase, inform me that she had had it with me, this ole cold, fallin' down farm, and that she was going back home to Mama, and she'd slam the door on the way out.

Most of the time she would only walk down to the corner with Hooker, sit on her suitcase for a couple thinking by now that I had learned my lesson, and then come back home. Sometimes she'd get her suitcase and go to a friends for an afternoon to try and really scare me into thinking I had lost her forever.

One time she actually made it all the way back to Tulsa. She spent three or four days there just to teach me a good lesson, until I wrote her a letter telling her how lonesome it was here on the farm. I said all the animals were saying to me how much they missed her. Wilbur the pig would say, "Where is our Charlie?" Blossom, the cow said, "I just can't stand how lonesome it is without Charlie." The same went for Hooker and the other animals.

In my letter I told her all the animals on the farm kept buggin' me and saying, "Lowell, you bastard, what have you done with our Charlie?" Also in the letter I told her how we loved and missed our Charlie. With that, we finally got her to come home again. This time she went upstairs, unpacked her suitcase, and put it in the attic. She never threatened to go home to Mama again.

That same winter, we had become friends with Danny Hensley. At first I think it was because he had a four wheel drive pickup. The snow was so heavy that year we couldn't get out our driveway, much less to the dirt road that ran east and west in front of the farm. The snow had blown over the road so bad that even the snow plow was stuck in front of our house for three days. I didn't think they were going to get it out until spring. Anyways, we would call good ole Danny and have him bring groceries in to us.

When Danny brought the groceries he would sit and watch me paint. Finally one day I painted a pair of bird dogs on point. This painting really flicked ole Danny's switch and he bought it from me. Well, that painting got him hooked on my originals. It seemed like Danny was out at our farm every other day, trying and buying every painting I turned out. He probably bought fifteen or twenty that winter. I must say we sure needed the money. But spring was coming and I had to get several paintings ready for my spring art show in the southeast.

So, I told Danny I couldn't sell him another painting until after that tour. But that didn't stop him from wanting to buy the cream of the paintings I was gathering up for the tour.

Again, Charlie and I loaded up the old Dodge car and the tent trailer with Hooker and headed for South Carolina and Florida.

On our return, again we took the money from the sales and fixed up another existing building. We hired a carpenter, Leonard Rose, to restore out fallen down barn. Leonard stayed with us as our full-time carpenter for eight years. He fixed up our house and out buildings and later built two new ones for us.

Charlie and I had a hobby. We would drove around country roads in all kinds of weather photographing old form houses, barns, outbuildings, vacant general stores, blacksmith's shops, deserted country schools and other buildings that dotted the countryside. It was so sad to see all those fallen down farms. I remember when they were all painted up, with orchards, gardens, and white fences. Now the grandson, or someone else, was using the old home place to raise pigs in while he lived down the road in a trailer house with a satellite dish. I knew those buildings would never get a new roof or another paint job, and ten years from now, there would be nothing left of them except for the daffodils that came up each spring to show us that at one time there had been life there. I tried to get all these buildings documented in one form or another. I would first photograph them and later they would become subject matter for many of my paintings.

The next year Charlie and I hit the art shows across the country from coast to coast. That summer we sold the Dodge and upgraded to a Volkswagen bus, some upgrade! We put three new engines in it within ten thousand miles. When the third engine went out, we just unloaded our belongings and left it on the side of the road in the mountains of Georgia. We hitchhiked to Atlanta airport and flew home. As far as I know, that Volkswagen bus is still sittin' there in Georgia on the side of the road.

We had met a lot of great artists at different shows that year and we kept in communication with them. At the same time, people in the Carthage area were asking me if I would give art lessons. My answer was always, "I would love to give art lessons, but I'm all but self taught and I ain't got the foggiest idea how to teach someone else how to draw or paint."

Danny decided to go to an art show with Charlie and me that summer when we asked him if he's like to go along. Also, two of my favorite artist's, Bob Tommey of Texas, and Ron Crooks of California, whom I was anxious to meet, were going to be there. Danny and I made and instant friendship with Bob and Ron. We even spent our evenings with them. That's when I found out that Bob was not only one of the greatest painters I'd ever met, but was also one of the greatest art teachers in the country.

So, a light bulb goes off in my head. Art teacher, people in Carthage are a were wanting art lessons, so , one night while we were all out to dinner, we worked out a plan for Bob and Ron to come to Carthage some time in December. Bob could give a week's art seminar and over the next weekend we would put on an art show like this area had never seen.

I remember when I first moved back to Carthage, I was approached by someone saying, "Lowell, no one could sell a painting in Carthage for more than $45.00 dollars," but I knew the only reason a painting wouldn't sell for more than $45.00 dollars was because very few people in the area had ever been exposed to art. It was our thinking that the art shows out west were always successful, so why couldn't an art show be successful here in the flatlands. Anyways, it was worth a try.

Danny and I came back to Carthage to set Bob up with a week long painting workshop. Then we set up a show the following weekend at the ole C&W Café on the Carthage Square. Also, there was a young want-to-be artist in South Carolina I had met at a show in Myrtle Beach. His name was Chris Leiter, and he had hit me up for art lessons. I liked the young man while I was there I did take time to go paint with him on location one afternoon. After all, I knew I could teach anyone all I knew about painting in that length of time.

When I found out that Bob was willing to come to Carthage and give a workshop, I called Chris and said to him, "Chris, to make up for my lack of knowledge on giving art lessons, have I got a deal for you! No matter what it takes ," I continued to him, "you need to be in

Carthage in December and take Bob's classes. Also , you might want to bring some of your paintings because after the classes we are going to put on an art show."

The art show was scheduled for a Friday night in December – and what a night it was! There were three inches of ice and snow on the ground. The weather couldn't have been worse, but the attendance and sales at the show couldn't have been better. It was a sell-out!

We enjoyed that night so much we said, "Hey, we gotta do this again next year and invite our favorite and best artists from all across the country." We did it again the next year and the next year and again the next, and that art show is still going on to this day. It's called the Midwest Gathering of the Arts.

Our next thought was to really expose people in the area to art, so we needed to put in a gallery so we could keep art alive all year long. That's when we opened the doors to the Flatlander Gallery on the Carthage Square.

Meanwhile, back on the far: By now Charlie and I had all the existing farm buildings up to their original condition. We had our Noah's Ark farm. A pair or more of every type of animal that ever lived on an American farm. We had work horses, mules, goats, sheep, cows, pigs, and lots and lots of chickens, duck, geese, and all the rest.

Up to this time I had still been painting and sculpting wildlife. Most of the time when I had painted large game animals I was faking it by using photographs. I'd never seen a grizzly bear except in a zoo. I'd never seen a moose closer than two hundred yards, but I did know farm animals inside and out. So, I started painting the subject matter around me. I did six farm animal bronzes and started painting the same subject matter.

Charlie and I started taking the farm animal paintings and bronzes to show, but on the way to our first showing in Denver, I kept thinking to myself, "Now, who would buy a painting of a cow or a sculpture of a pig?" The answer, "Nobody" I'd never seen then at any art show or hanging in any gallery. Then I got to thinking how western paintings and bronzes were sold in the west and then I thought, "Hey! There are more people raised on farms than there ever was raised on a ranch. Maybe they will sell."

Well, sell they did! I sold out all my farm animal paintings and bronzes in a matter of a couple of hours. The response was overwhelming. I was so excited on our drive back to Missoura; I said to Charlie, "Honey, I'm on to something." I also told her how I felt I had pioneered the wildlife art in Texas, but when other artists saw my success with wildlife, a lot of them jumped on the bandwagon and started painting and sculping the same thing and it got completely away from me.

They passed me up like I was standing still and "I don't want that to happen this time." I also told her when we got home that I was going to sculpt farm animals and try to put a figurine line together.

I did just that. I sculpted twelve different subjects: Chickens, cows, pigs, goats, and so on, but now that I had them sculpted, how was I going to market them?

Then I decided to get in touch with Kaiser of Kaiser Porcelain Company in Germany, but a couple of years earlier, as I was going through my divorce, I had told them to shove our contract, so I didn't have the balls to call him up and ask for his forgiveness. And with that in mind, I called my old friend Jerry Cooper in Atlanta, the man from my Grey Period. I asked if he could set me up a meeting with Hubert to show him my new line, and see if he would produce them like my wildlife porcelains. A few weeks later, Jerry called and said the Kaisers were going to be in the United States in three weeks. They had reluctantly agreed to meet me in Savannah, Georgia, to see the new line.

Jerry also invited Charlie and me to stay in his cabin in the Georgia mountains for a week before our arranged meeting.

We stayed in his cabin and we were to meet with the Kaiser's on a Friday night at 7 o'clock in a certain Savannah restaurant. We had a six hour drive from that cabin to Savannah We were running late Friday morning but if we drove exactly the speed limit and didn't have any problems, we could just make it to the restaurant on time.

Well, I did better on our speed. I mean out tires were squallin' around every Georgia mountain curve and I had the pedal to the metal on the straight-aways, determined not to miss that appointment.

Jerry Cooper had said he had gone so far as to buy Mrs. Kaiser a new fur coat, just to sweeten up the ante.

Well, about ten minutes to five we were going through a little Georgia town called Etonton, when low and behold, bigger than Dallas, was the Brer Rabbit Museum. I slammed on the brakes and pulled into the parking lot. I said to Charlie, "Honey, I just gotta go thru this museum." Brer Rabbit, Brer Fox, Uncle Remus, they were my heroes growing up. My grade school teachers read it to us at recess if it was raining outside. "I know we will be running late, because Savannah is still two hours away, but I just have to do this, " I declared. "I'll just run through it in five minutes."

I was walking though the museum as fast as I could, just glancing from side to side, soaking up everything, like I had a radar. That is, until I got to the end, and there was rooms decorated just like the inside of Uncle Remus' cabin. And this little ole lady was sitting behind a counter, in a rocking chair by a fireplace. On the counter was Joe Chandler Harris' book on the tales of Uncle Remus, illustrated by my favorite illustrator, A.B. Frost. I had wanted this book forever, but it was banned from schools, libraries and book stores across America. I started digging money out of my pockets as fast as I could and told the lady in the rocking chair I wanted to buy that book.

When she came up to the counter to ring up the book, I noticed she had the sweetest little southern voice I had ever heard. I asked her, "Do you read Uncle Remus?" And in that little southern accent, she said, "Well, I sure do. I was a school teacher for thirty years." I said, "Well, would you mind, beings it's closing time, to just read me a little bit?" Again, she said, "Sure."

Charlie and I pulled our chairs up beside her. We were so enthralled with the flow of her accent in reading; it was like the most beautiful music I had ever heard. Two hours later, at 7 o'clock, we came out of our trance. I was in shock, and said, "Charlie, we've missed our dinner engagement with the Kaiser's."

We picked up our newly acquired book and went back out to the parking lot. We were sitting in our car, trying to figure out what to do next, and I said, "You screw a German around twice and you don't get a third shot. German's are that way." I didn't see much point in trying to schedule another appointment with the Kaiser's. So with that in mind, we turned the car around and headed back to Missoura.

A lot of things happened in that year of 1976, the Bicentennial Year. Charlie and I had our first Child, a son named Peter Jeb.

April, my oldest daughter, moved from Texas and her mother, to live with us. Soroptimist International of Carthage commissioned me to paint an 8 foot by 30 foot mural of the history of Carthage and Jasper County. The mural would be placed in the Jasper County Courthouse in Carthage as a Bicentennial gift to the people of the area.

The chairman of the Project was Dallie Miessner, Lifestyles Editor at the Carthage Press. We got to know Dallie as a friend during those months I worked on the mural.

During dedication ceremony, I felt someone patting me on the back. I turned to see who it was and found it was Miss Emma Metsker, who had paid my way through my art classes some twenty five years earlier.

Also, that same year, we had several out buildings moved to the farm. Every time I drove through the countryside, I would see and old corn crib, a privy, or chicken house that was falling down. I would ask the farmer, who owned it, if I could have the building. Then move it back to our farm and fix and paint it up to it's original grandeur.

All the time these things were happening, I was doing my art work and in the fall of 1976 I was determined to find another distributor to handle my new line. Beings that I had been in the gift business before with Kaiser, I already had a toe-hold into that business and I was familiar with different distributing companies.

With this in mind, I decided the first company I would call on would be the biggest and best. So, the first one I called was Schmid, out of Randolph, Massachusetts, near Boston, and I asked to speak to Victor Noel, senior vice president of marketing. When I got Victor on the phone, I told him the reason for my call and said I had designed a new Uncle Remus line. I was headed for the New England area, because that's the area where the headquarters of the four largest distributors in the nation were located. I told him I would like to call on Schmid while I was in the area. Victor, who was familiar with my work and my name, said, "Would you mind calling on us first?" And that's just what I did!

# Chapter 5

**Hooker. Lowell's "Dollar Dog" and #1 Model**

**Schmid** – The Good Years:

One of the main reasons I was so excited about running across the Brer Rabbit Museum that day I Georgia, was that I already started sculpting a series of six Uncle Remus figurines. The day I went through the museum, I had already completed four of the six figurines, so as soon as we returned from that trip, I finished the other two.

There was Brer Rabbit, Brer Bear, Brer Wolf, Brer Weasel, Brer Fox, and Brer Coyote. I packed those 6 figurines, plus 6 larger farm animal figurines, and 6 small farm animal figurines and caught a flight outta Joplin for Boston. I intended to sell Schmid my Brer series. I had the other twelve figurines to show them I was more versatile than just doing cartoon type characters.

As soon as I entered Schmid's offices I was escorted to a conference room. I unpacked my little sculptures and laid them out on the conference table. Than, all the key executives, including Victor Noel, stood around "oohing" and "awing" over the farm animals. They didn't say much about the Brer series because they were afraid the series had racial overtones. I said, "Hey, us southern boys cut our teeth on Uncle Remus. I know they will go over in the south."

"We'll take and produce the farm animals, but we wont touch the Remus characters," they said. I replied, "No deal" and started packing up my figurines. I got real ballsie and said to them, "Who is the nest best gift distributor in the area?"

Finally, reluctantly, they said, "Okay, if we can sign you up to a contract, we will produce the Brer Series."

Then they asked me what medium could I see them produced in? I said, "I don't know, bronze? Pewter? Traditional porcelain?" None of these mediums excited me too much, but at the time those were the only materials I thought were available. Then Victor said, "Come with me" and escorted me back to their vault. He showed me four small wildlife and bird figurines. He handed me one and said, "Do you know what material these are cast in?" "No" I answered, "But they are beautiful!"

"It's called cold cast porcelain," he said. Then Victor told me the story of a young English inventor who lived in Scotland that had discovered a new process and had brought these four pieces over to Schmid only two weeks prior to my visit. Victor than asked, "Would you consider having your figurines cast in this material?" I started asking him questions about shrinkage, colors fading, etc. He said, "Wait, lets go into my office and call him. His name is John Hammond." I had been working in traditional porcelain where there is a lot of do's and don'ts. There is a 17 percent shrinkage problem. That not only means the size would come down by 17 percent, but also detail would shrink out. Therefore, the artist has to exaggerate everything when sculpting a piece. For example, if you are sculpting a bird, and the bird has a wing sticking out, if you turn the wing one way, it might only take two molds for the wing. If the wing is turned another way, it might take up to 6 molds to cast the wing.

There are a lot more problems the sculptor has to contend with in working with traditional porcelain, like will the colors fade in the firing? All of these questions I wanted to ask John Hammond. John told me over the phone that none of these questions created a problem for him, although in traditional porcelain, the artist is a slave to the medium. He informed me that anything the artist did, they could cast. In fact, he told me I could sculpt as difficult as I wanted, be cause he loved the challenge.

After Victor and I hung up the phone, Victor told me John had named his company Border Fine Arts and that it was located in the Border District of Scotland, just north of the English border. He said John had just started the company and had brought the figurines in the vault to them as samples.

I was so excited about the whole concept. Schmid was taking me on and distributing my work to gift shops across the country, I got my way with the Brer Series, and I was going to have my figurines cast in a brand new medium that other artist didn't even know about.

Victor kept my figurines and said he was going to ship them to Scotland immediately. He said for me to go home and he would have a contract in the mail to me in a few days. He also advised me to tell my wife to get packed, because as soon as Border Fine Arts had made molds of my figurines, we would go to Scotland so I could paint the first copies. Then, their master painters could reproduce them, exactly as I wanted them.

Victor took me to the airport, we shook hands on the deal, and after that, Border Fine Arts, Schmid, and Lowell Davis had a perfect marriage. I'll tell you what, I was on such a high when Victor let me off at the airport, I could have flown home even without an airplane.

About a month later, Charlie and I went to Scotland. The Schmid representatives were cream of the cream, Cadillac of gift sales reps.

We introduced the line in 1978 at the Gift Mart in Atlantic City, New Jersey. One of the biggest shows in the country, it's held each January. It was a huge success with Schmid promoting my line as "COUNTRY IS IN!" During the Gift Mart, hundreds of artists were there with hundreds and thousands of gift distributors showing their wares. It was such a large show it took gift buyers three or four days to go through the entire show. But, they had to see everything there was to choose from so they would know what to buy to sell in their gift shops back home.

While I was at the show, I tried to make it around to all the distributors boots. I was looking for anything that might have a country theme, nothing! Not one thing that depicted country, but then, at that time, the only thing on the market having anything to do with country was country music.

There were no country magazines, and country crafts hadn't raised its ugly head in those days! I was the first one to come out with anything that had to do with country. I guess that's why they later dubbed me the "Grandfather of Country Art."

The Schmid sales reps were so busy at that show writing orders they thought their hands were going to fall off. To me, it was like I was one of the forty year overnight success stories.

Now I was making enough money so that I was able to really fix up my farm. I moved in more outbuildings. Finally, a neighbor came over and said, "Lowell, if you bring another building onto this place it's goin' to sink." The only problem with having our farm all fixed up is that I never got to stay home and enjoy it!

Now things were going so well. Schmid wanted me out on the road promoting and introducing the line. It was fun at first, going to gift shops from coast to coast, and every city and town in between, I would be away from home as much as 6 weeks at a time.

In those days, I might be in Birmingham, Alabama, one night and get up early the next morning for a television interview, then a radio interview, a newspaper interview and then spend four hours at a gift shop, meeting people and signing figurines for all my collectors. The next morning I'd fly out of Birmingham to somewhere like Omaha, and the next day it all started all over again.

I always loved meeting the collectors, but after several years of flying, airports, television and newspaper interviews all the fun went out of it.

Schmid always flew me first class. The gift shop folks always wanted to take me to first class restaurants and Schmid always put me up in the first class hotels near the airport.

Now that I am on the subject of the title of this book, I would like to elaborate on first class and what first class really means to me.

It means you don't dare talk to the person setting next to you because they sure as hell don't want to talk to you. After flying in first class a couple of year, I requested Schmid fly me coach. The folks are a little bit friendlier back there. Mot much, but a little friendlier.

I remember one time I was flying from St. Louis to Los Angeles. After we were airborne for an hour or so, I said something, or asked a question of the man seated beside me. He just grunted and answered my question with a couple of words. Then he picked up a book and started, or played like, he was reading.

We flew on another hour and a half or so, all the time me just staring at the back of the seat in front of me. When we started dropping altitude into Los Angeles airport, I couldn't stand it any longer. I turned to the man again and said, "Sir, I really hate to bother you again, but I just gotta ask you a question. Now, if you were walking down a country dirt road headed to town and it was a two and a half hour walk, and this guy on a wagon pulled by a team of mules stops and says, "Hey, buddy, you want a ride to town?" and you say, "Sure" and he then says, "Well, jump on the tailgate." Then he pops the reins and the mules take off, plodding down the dirt road to town, and you just sit back there on the tailgate staring off into the countryside. Not long after he picks you up, he comes upon another fellow walking down that dirt road to town. The driver stops and asks him the same thing. The fellow says, "Sure." The driver tells him, "Well, jump on the tailgate with that other fellow."

I looked at the guy sitting next to me on that flight and asked, "You mean to tell me those two fellows are going to sit back on that tailgate, starring off into space and not talk to each other for two and a half hours?" The man grunted and stuck his nose in his book again, and I just sat there for the rest of the flight and starred at the back of the seat in front on me.

See, folks, there ain't no memories in First Class.

Now, when I drove my ole 1932 wooden motor home I call the Leapin' Lizard across the country, everybody talked to me. Sometimes it would take me an hour to fill the Leapin' Lizard with gas and thirty minutes extra just to walk out of a restaurant or café.

When I'd pull into a campsite, forget it! At two in the morning, I would have to stand up, stretch and yawn, and say to the folks sitting there talking to me, "Well, I think it's about time we pissed on the fire and called in the dogs."

In those first class hotel like the Adams Mark, Sheridan's, Hilton's etc., can you imagine seeing a couple of men in suits and ties, with their little briefcases, and you walk up to them and say, "Hi guys. What's happening?" and sit down next to them and try to have a conversation? I'll tell you, there ain't no memories in First Class!

During all those years I spent hundred and hundreds of nights in sterile hotel rooms where I'd be on the 30th floor and couldn't even open a window! Give me an old 1950's motel anytime. You know, in all those nights, in all those fancy rooms, I don't have one good memory.

Give me a motel where you can park your car outside your room, go inside and throw open the windows.

I have tons of wonderful memories of Charlie, Hooker, and I traveling cross country in that ole beat up Dodge car and that Mickey Mouse tent trailer. Like the night we were camped out in a snow storm and a wind came up while we were sleeping. It blew the tent part off out trailer and Charlie had a hell of a time trying to get that tent cover back on by herself while I lay snug in my sleeping bag. And then, the times we would get up on a cold morning and the coffee pot would be frozen to the grill. Now, those are great memories.

Anyway, it was about this time, while I was working with Schmid that I ran across the Leapin' Lizard. I then told Schmid that the Lizard was the only way I wanted to travel from then on.

Let me explain what the Leapin' Lizard is and how I came about acquiring her. I was over at Bill Snow's, and artist friend in Carthage. We were working on something in his back yard and I asked for a screw driver. He motioned to an ole shed, covered with tim, and said, "There's one just inside the door."

I opened the door to the tin shed and stepped inside. There were no windows and the only light was coming in through the open door. I stood there letting my eyes adjust to the darkness, and then I saw ribs in the ceiling. The dash and the old steering wheel started coming into focus. There were boxes and junk scattered all over the rest of the shed. I stepped back into the daylight and hollered, "Hey, Bill! What is this thing?"

**The Leapin' Lizard**

## THE LEAPIN' LIZARD:

Bill walked over to where I was standing, stepped inside with me and explained. "It's an ole 1930 Medicine Man's motor home."

"Well, what are you going to do with it?" I asked. Bill said he'd had good intentions of restoring it for the past twenty years, but now, he realized he was never going to get around to it. He had been using it for a storage shed, but now it was in his way and he was going to light a match to it!

I asked, "Well, could I have it?" He said "Sure, if you hurry up and come get it outta my way." With that, said he had to go into town. I asked, "Do you mind if I just stay here and study this thing?" Bill said, "help yourself. I'll be back in about twenty minutes, if your still here."

It started to rain, The old motor home had been covered with tin and the sound of the rain on that ole tin roof held me spellbound. Even the windows had been covered over with tin, and I guess it musta been the tine that saved her all those years.

With the door open to allow light to come through and the rain falling on the tin roof, I just sat there and looked around. "She's all here." I thought to myself, the bed, the cabinets and the dash. A lot of the old wood was rotted and at one time a tree limb had fallen across the roof and crashed in a couple of roof ribs and the door. The front end had been cut off back to the firewall, so there was no engine. Otherwise, it was all there. Anyways, there was enough to get a pattern off if it., so I could replace any broken boards. I started moving boxes around so I could get a better visual. I lifted up the linoleum and under it were wooden floors covered with old newspapers of the same vintage as the old motor home. I picked up one of those papers, the comic strips, of course, and carried it over to the open door where the light was better. I was reading "Little Orphan Annie," and she said, "Leapin' Lizards." Now, I'd been wanting to restore something like a car ot an old pickup every since I was a kid and never got around to it, but by golly, this time I was going to do it! I was going to restore this thing and when I do, I'm going to name her the "Leapin' Lizard."

I finally got her transported back to the farm. Our carpenter, Leonard Rose, who had been building and restoring all our old buildings, up to that time, had always bragged that he could restore any building or house that I brought home. I'd brought him many challenges, but when I brought home the Lizard, Leonard said, "Lowell, you've brought me some real doozies, but I'll have to admit, this is going to be the ultimate challenge." Then he said, "I'm goin' to have to scratch my head on this one."

After Leonard ripped out all the rotten and broken boards he went through the process of replacing them until it was exactly like it was when it had been built a half century earlier.

About the time Leonard had completed all the wood structure a friend and collector of my figurines, Ray Pittman, of Kansas City, was down at the farm for a visit. I proudly showed Ray the Lizard and said, "All the wood work is done. Now I only have one problem, There's no front end and no motor." I told him I was looking for an old truck chassis to mount the wooden box on.

Now, Ray had a big business in Olathe, Kansas, called R.O. Corporation, dealing with trucks, cranes, and lifts. He said to me, "Lowell, let the men in my company do it for you. I've got a 2-ton truck chassis and an engine that has very low mileage that we can drop her on. I also have engineers that will get it mounted correctly. I'm afraid if you do it, you might have her driving down the road sideways."

A short time later, Jim Frerer, a good friend, volunteered to haul it to Olathe on his flat bed trailer.

Within four months the Lizard was ready to roll. Now, my only problem was that what I had was a big wooden box with a naked engine sticking out in front. No lights, no grill, no fenders, nothing, just wheels and engine. So, my next step was to find the best auto body man in the area to start the complex job of building a front end.

We used Model "A" Ford fenders, '27 Chevrolet head lights, a 1932 Ford Radiator Cover, firewall and cowling, with a Freightliner grill. Everything had to be greatly enlarged to fit over that big 460 Ford engine and radiator. After a couple of months the Leapin' Lizard was finally completed and really ready to roll. Leonard's beautiful wooden box and Jim's front end. What a beauty!

Now she was really ready for the road. Just about the time the Lizard was completed, Schmid scheduled two, two week tours from Arkansas to North Dakota and all the stops in between.

Charlie had just finished decorating the inside the night before the lizard's maiden voyage. I was so excited I couldn't sleep. I just lie there in bed with my eyes open, waiting for the crack of dawn. Finally, it was daylight and time for me to take off. Charlie and all my family was there to wish me and Hooker "bon voyage."

Now, I do try to stay humble and try never to be a proud man, but that morning as I was cruising west on ole Highway 96, headed for Wichita, for my first tour stop, I was one proud puppy.

Me and my dog Hooker in the Leapin' Lizard, with the C.B. on, listening to the truckers talking about us, trying to figure out what the hell I was. That day was the start of a long and wonderful relationship with the Lizard.

I've put seventy thousand miles on the Lizard. She has been to forty two of the lower forty eight states and she's like driving a barn down the road. After four or five hours of driving her, I'd be worn out and have to shut her down. That's why when I did most of my touring, Schmid usually had a driver go with me.

Charlie never wanted to go with me in the Leapin' Lizard because she was always too embarrassed, and if she did go, when we pulled into a restaurant, she'd make me park out in the back so she wouldn't be seen getting out of it.

I have many fond memories of the travels and adventures of me and the Lizard touring back and forth, upside down and backward, across the country, visiting gift shops and department stores, meeting collectors all across this good ole U.S. of A, but that would be another book!

# Chapter 6

**Red Oak II**

## RED OAK II:

By now I was on top of the world. November 11, 1979, Charlie blessed me with another child. This time it was the cutest little baby girl. We named her Jenny Wren.

The farm was completely restored. There was no more room to bring in or build another building.

I had big plans for turning my farm into a self sufficient farm museum. I was making so much money off the sales of my porcelain figurines I didn't know what to do with it. I always said "I'm not into Mercedes, swimming pools or villas in France."

It was about this time I would catch myself staring over the fence at the big field just east of the house. As an artist, I kept looking at that field as if it were a big blank canvas. I had seen farm artists that plant different crops in designs and patterns to form a picture in their field that you could see from the air. I have a lot of admiration for those artists and I love their works of art. So, this field would be my statement in art. I decided to do it with buildings and sculptures and my medium would be old buildings. Buildings that I could relate to in their architectural form.

The first building I brought in for my art statement was the Feed and Seed store. It was restored on a lot. I put it right next to the farm, in case hard times would hit, or something would happen to me, and Charlie might want to open an antique shop, sell eggs and milk, or something like that. I built it before I had any concept of building a town.

The second building was the Elmira country school house. It was a real basket case when I found her. Sam Butcher, the creator of Precious Moments and I were driving around on country roads one day when we saw an old deserted school house. We stopped in, went in, and talked about how it should be saved. The windows were out, the roof was half gone, and the floors were rotted out from years of farmers storing hay in it.

It was sure an exciting day when Oran Tilton's house moving service brought the old, run-down Elmira in and set her out in the middle of that ten acres. It just sat there, waiting for me to earn enough money to restore it. Then Sam came by and gave me $10,000.00 dollars to have it done.

Oh, how beautiful she was all restored inside, with the new bell tower on top. When we finally got a fresh coat of white paint on her and with the sun shining off her, she looked like a beautiful prairie flower out in the middle of that green field.

I was on a real high and I think that's what really gave me the bug to restore more old buildings. The third building to be moved in was the most important one. The Red Oak General Store. The one my parents had lived in during the war. It was the building all my ancestors, on both sides of the family had visited and traded in since the pioneer days of Red Oak.

It, too, was in bad shape but would have never have gotten another new roof or another coat of pain. After we had restored the old building and all the old antique fixtures on the inside and restocked all the shelves, Sam drives up and honks. I go out to his car and he says, "get in." Then he drove back to Precious Moments and here is this cute little gingerbread house.

Sam had just purchases the land around it and said if I wanted it for Red Oak II, he would have it moved to the farm. I said, "Sure, Sam. I never turn down any contribution offered to Red Oak II from anyone."

I told Sam it was an exact replica of my great-grandma Weber's house in Red Oak. After it was moved to its present site, Sam said to me, "Lowell, beings it's going to be the Red Oak II schoolmarm's house I had an art teacher in high school, Mr. Morivac, I would like to pay for its restoration and dedicate it to him."

So, that's how the schoolmarm's house came about. Again, thanks to Sam Butcher. For it was Sam who had saw my dream and paid for the first two building in Red Oak II, which was now starting to look like a town. Not that I ever meant for it to be a town.

It was to me a piece of art that just happened to look like a town. Every building was to be a piece of art. There would be no Formica, no plastic, all of my art material would be something that someone else had thrown away. Everything had to go back to its original form, except for the slight changes in my architectural design. Even down to each of the buildings stone foundations. All the stone work had to be a piece of art. I never went over to Red Oak II and asked any of the carpenters or stone mason's, "How much did you get done today?" I only demanded they be proud of what they had accomplished at the end of the day, because they were all going to sign their names to the finished project.

My grandfather's blacksmith's shop was the next building to be moved in from the old Red Oak.

Leonard Rose was the carpenter that built and restored most of our farm and was my foreman, responsible for the first buildings in Red Oak II. Later on, during the Red Oak II project, Rick Hood and his brother Billy we overseers of all the construction on the buildings. All the beautiful stone work at Red Oak II was done by a stone mason named Joe McNelly. He was a real artist with stone and the stone work of Red Oak II is a monument to his career and his talent.

If a teacher thinks he or she doesn't make a difference in a child's like, think of Sam and Mr. Morivac or myself and Miss Metsker.

# Chapter 7
# Schmid

**DEMISE OF SCHMID**:

Red Oak II was beginning to look like a town. We had a general store, country school, blacksmith's shop, and a couple of house. All we need was a church. All this time, of course, I had been telling Charlie that every building I bought "would be the last!" Actually, there were no deserted churches in our area. Most of them only had handfuls of people left in their congregations, but none of them were actually closed.

But, just six miles north of our farm there was the neatest little country church, Salem Church. There were no more than eight or ten people who regularly attended. I had approached them earlier to say if they ever closed the church doors, I would be interested in moving it to Red Oak II. I had also approached a couple of the other little country churches in the area and made them the same offer, but there were no takers. About a year after I made the offer on Salem Church a member called me and said, "Lowell, we had a meeting of the minds last Sunday. We came to the realization. Our roof leaks and there's no money in our budget for repairs, so, if you would enclose the little annex off the side, you can have the main church."

That little church is now standing proudly in Red Oak II. We have services in it every Sunday night and alls welcome. Not to worry, I don't preach!

By now my royalties from Schmid were at their peak. I could have three or four buildings moved and restored at a time. Schmid sales were soaring! But bad times were on the way.

Schmid had won a long drawn-out lawsuit with Gobel of Germany. The makers of Hummel figurines. Schmid was the sole distributor of the Hummel figurine line, but Gobel put all types of demands and restrictions on Schmid that later proved to be their downfall. One of Gobel's demands was that Schmid divide their sales and office force in half. I knew then that I was going to turn into a stepchild.

At the time Schmid had four major figurine lines. Hummel, Lowell Davis, Anri and Disney. The court decision called for Schmid to be cut into two divisions, with Anri and me making up the Schmid Division and Hummel and Disney making up the Hummel Division.

Up to that time, Bob Lytle was the preacher at the Red Oak II church. He had asked in one of his sermons, "Is there anyone in this congregation who doesn't have problems? Or anyone who has never had problems?" Well, I had never had problems in my life except for my divorce, but I didn't want to be the only one to hold up my hand. But, from that moment on, my life changed. After that, when Brother Bob asked that question, I could jump on my seat and vigorously wave both hands in the air! But back to my story.

Another of Gobel's demands was that Schmid guarantee to purchase millions of dollars worth of Hummel products each year, whether they sold or not. Of course those sales weren't nearly as high as Schmid had anticipated and Schmid has signed the contract.

Another demand Gobel made was that Schmid had to have a huge advertising and promotional budget, devoted solely to their product. But Hummel sales were getting worse and worse and Schmid had warehouses full of Hummel figurines. Millions of dollars were tied up with Hummel.

Now Schmid didn't have the money to spend on the advertising budget that was in the contract, Soooo! Where was Schmid going to come up with the money? You guessed it! They looked over into the Schmid Division, i.e. Lowell Davis budget, and said, "Wow! This Lowell Davis figurine line is highly successful," and they decided to raise the price of the Lowell Davis figurine line and take those profits to help them get outta their Hummel hole.

So, jack up the prices they did. In some cases, three or four times. Schmid also took the Anri and Lowell Davis advertising and promotional budgets and put that into their Hummel-Disney Division. Schmid even got into gimmickry, and for the first time in my career I was ashamed of the work with my name on it.

They wre whoring my work! They would sell out an entire addition of one of my figurines lines, and all the collectors thought if a certain figurine was sold out, maybe their investment would go up, wrong! Schmid would crank up the molds and have a few hundred run off. By making some minor alteration in the painting of a figurine, or some molding change.

Then they started raising the numbers of the edition. They must have been thinking that my collectors were stupid or something. I kept telling Schmid, "Hey! My collectors know more about what's happening to Lowell Davis line and about me, more about me than I know myself.

You ain't goin' to pull the wool over their eyes." But bad went to worse, and Schmid's went into Chapter Eleven. Well, I always say there are two things that will destroy any business and that I greed and ego. Those two factors sure played a big role in Schmid's demise.

Now, I loved and was proud to have been associated with Schmid and sixteen of those years had been the greatest! Now they were in trouble. This was no time to get angry, and I knew, as bad as I hated being on the road, no matter what the cost or how much I had to be on the road, it had to be done.

For more than sixty years, Schmid has been the Cadillac of the gift distributors. Now they were headed south. I had to put every effort I could into trying to prevent a Schmid bankruptcy.

Jerry Truman, one of my biggest collectors, was from Minnesota. He was a retired businessman and had a big interest in saving the line, and the major investment he had in all my figurines. He also knew it was going to be rough on me to handle the big tour schedule Schmid bestowed upon me. So Jerry told Schmid if they paid his expenses, he would go on the road and help me drive the Leapin' Lizard. Well, we literally put thousands and thousands of miles on the Lizard that last year. From the east coast to the state of Washington, and all down the west coast. Like having shows all the way down to L.A. and then over to Arizona and back to Missoura. That totaled up to about 6 weeks.

With all the tours that last year, plus the fact that I could see my 40-year art career going down the toilet, and keeping in mind the thousands and thousands of collectors that had invested their hard-earned money in me. I felt like I was letting them down.

At the end of that trying year I went to the office one day and picked up my mail and there it was, Schmid's bankruptcy! I had felt it was coming, so I had contacted Enesco Distributors, another gift distributor, for in my contract it stated if Schmid ever went into bankruptcy it would terminate the contract. I would be free to go to Enesco, or any other gift distributor, but wrong again!

The bankruptcy court had tied up Schmid's assets, and of course, Lowell Davis was one of those assets. This meant I was not going to be paid anymore royalties from Schmid, plus, I couldn't go with another company. But the worse part of the whole deal was that Schmid put a gag order on me. Meaning I couldn't tell anybody, collectors or anyone, anything about anything.

During that last year on the road, I knew all the time that Schmid had this huge inventory of millions and millions for dollars worth of inventory in their warehouses.

Under pressure from bankers, Schmid really started whoring and prostituting my figurine line. They would have people in the home office sign my books and my figurines to help boost sales. Then, they decided to have this plowing under program. That meant they would get rid of their excessive inventory. They would give my collectors one last chance to buy a bunch of them, and the ones that didn't sell by a certain date, they were going to have me plow them all under. I went along with their scheme, but very reluctantly.

When the deadline came they promised the collectors they were going to plow them under and they did send Loretta, the lady in charge of the Lowell Davis Farm Club, down with some token pieces with me on the plow behind the tractor for a photo opportunity.

They told me they only sent down a few token pieces because otherwise it would take several 18-wheelers to bring them all the way from Boston, which was a blatant lie to me collectors. What they did was discount the figurines out the back door to clearing houses at 10 cents on the dollar.

Now, for all those collectors who had invested in my art, and must have paid, let's say, $100.00 dollars for a piece, they would go into a gift shop and see the same piece on sale for half that price.

The only good thing that came out of this excess inventory is that it forced the prices down on my figurines and this made them more affordable which allowed a great many more new collectors to begin collecting those figurines.

**Burning studio**

BURNING MY STUDIO:

I guess, if I had to say what the reason behind me burning my studio was. It was a combination of strain of being on the road so much, the lying that went on behind my back to my collectors, and finding out Schmid still had millions more dollars of my figurines in warehouses, and were going to dump even more of them on the market. Also the first signs of divorce was looming on the horizon.

I had taken a financial blood bath for a year without one penny coming in, and worse of all, I kept seeing the faces of all those thousands of my collectors out there across the country. The little girl from New Orleans that baby sat to make enough money to buy my figurines. The blind girl from Seattle that collected my pieces. The lady from Denver that lived in a basement so she could save up and buy most of my pieces, and all the other collectors.

I guess I just snapped. That morning I walked out to my studio and sat down at my drawing board and stared out the window. On my drawing board were two letters. One was a contract to go to work for Enesco, all I had to do was reach over and sign the contract and they would send me $300,000.00 dollars up front money. On the other side of my drawing board was the Schmid lawsuit, stating I wasn't getting any more money from them, even though I hadn't been paid in a year, and I couldn't sign up with another company for another year and a half, until my contract with Schmid expired.

I guess the stress that was building up inside of me exploded. I picked up the Schmid bankruptcy papers and the unsigned Enesco contract, took my lighter and lit them. I opened the closet door in my studio, which housed hundreds of my drawings and a lot of my original paintings, and laid the flaming contracts on all my work. Without taking anything out of my studio, I walked out the door and headed over to Red Oak II, to one of our bed and breakfast houses.

I them made a pot of coffee, poured a cup, sat in an easy chair and looked out the window, watching the smoke barreling up from my studio. Later a fire truck drove up and then an ambulance pulled up at the house where I was having my coffee. I knew someone in my family had called it for me, so I walked out to the ambulance, got in, and they took me to the hospital.

When my doctor arrived he could see I had severe physical exhaustion. He told me what I needed more than anything was to stay in the hospital for thee or four days and get some rest.

With that advice, he gave me a shot for my nerves. Normally, that shot wouldn't have had any effect on 99% of the people who received it, but I am allergic to any kind of medication. I can't even take an Excedrin without it causing some type of reaction.

I fell asleep and I don't remember a thing after that. Four days later Charlie told me what happened. She said I got up out of my hospital bed, called one of the carpenters, and said, "Pick me up in front of the hospital." I walked in the house, without anyone around to notice that I had come home, then I got a .38 revolver and went into the den. I remember there was a fire going in the fireplace when I placed that revolver under my chin.

About that time, April and Charlie came into the house. They had heard I had wandered out of the hospital and a workman had brought me home. They were looking for me to find out why I had come home from the hospital three days early.

When they saw me in the den with the gun to my head and this glazed expression on my face, Charlie ran out the door to a neighbor's house and called the sheriff. April, my oldest daughter, sat beside me, crying and begging me not to go through with this terrible thing. Finally she succeeded in talking me out of the gun. They told me later the sheriff had come out to the farm and transported me over to Ozark Mental Health Center, in Joplin. The only thing I remember was waking up in the loony bin. I woke up not knowing where I was or how I got there. All I knew is that I woke up in a sterile room wearing nothing more than a little green gown and house slippers. Finally, a doctor came in and he told me what I had done.

I was 56 years old then and out of all those years the thought of suicide never crossed my mind, and hasn't again since that day.

I don't know what caused me to react the way I did unless it was an allergic reaction to the shot they had given me for my nerves. After being in that ward for a few days a worse case of paranoia set in. Big Time! I just knew the entire world had turned against me. I didn't trust my wife, any of my kids, friends, collectors, nobody!

I had three psychiatrists giving me test after test. None of them thought I was crazy, but that I was stressed completely out. They also thought I had a bad case of paranoia.

One psychiatrist did say to me, "Lowell, your not crazy, but it's not normal for an artist to burn down his studio!" I said to him, "Doc, I've been accused of a lot of things in my life, but I've never been accused of being normal."

Paranoia was so bad during those days at the clinic I didn't want any friends or any family members, not even my wife, to visit me, I thought they had all turned against me.

I did allow Jerry Truman to come over, more or less, to fine out what was going on at home.

What I did find out is that during the time I was at the Ozark Mental Health Center, Jerry Truman had convinced my family that I was really crazy and need much more help than they could give me in Joplin.

I also found out that when a person is going through a serious depression they think their enemies are their friends and their friends are their enemies.

Jerry felt I should be transferred to the State mental hospital in Springfield, Missoura, for more check ups, and he wanted me put on a medication called Lithium.

Well, after test after test, and with three different psychiatrists giving me a clean bill of health, Jerry still talked my family into entering me in a two week program and also volunteered to drive me to the Springfield hospital. He also convinced the staff at the Ozark Mental Health Center of the same thing. The only way I could get out of the Ozark Center a couple of days early was to promise them I would allow Jerry to drive me to Springfield and check myself in. I promised.

The staff at Ozark Mental Health said they were letting me out of the center two days earlier than my scheduled release so if I didn't keep my promise, they would put me in another loony bin for thirty days.

Well, I allowed Jerry to drive me to Springfield. I did as I promised and checked myself in. Then I took off running down the hall of that loony bin and I ran out the front door into the snow storm. I ran down the street and into an alley where I hid behind a dumpster, standing and shivering in about six inches of snow. As I was hiding behind that dumpster, freezing to death, I could hear people out looking for me.

I waited until I thought the coast was clear and walked to a Chinese Restaurant. I ordered a cup of won ton soup and a cup of coffee to warm me up. I sat there and contemplated my next move. I knew that by now, the whole world was out looking for me. I f I got caught, I was looking at thirty days in that state run clinic back in Joplin. That's where they put the bad cases, I had no intention of ending up there. As I needed to pay to get out of the restaurant, I remembered I had stuck a $100.00 dollar bill in my secret compartment of my belt, a long time ago, for an emergency. Well, this was an emergency!

Then, I went to a phone booth and called a cab company and asked how much it would cost for fare to Carthage. It was sixty miles and they told me in this snowstorm it would be ninety dollars. After paying for the soup and coffee, I said, "I'll take it. But not a penny more." I had only $2.75 left.

On the way back to Carthage that night, I tried to think where would be the best place to have the cab drop me off. I knew Jerry had made it back to my house and told my family that he ha been right! By my escaping I had confirmed that fact. By now, my paranoia was full blown. I couldn't think at that time. I didn't know if I could trust my kids. Finally, I decided I would go to Heather's, my middle daughter. The cab dropped me to her house in town, getting there about midnight.

Heather was still awake and said she had already heard the news of my escape. She was worried sick. I told her not to tell a soul, but I was going to hide out at her house until I could figure out what to do. I was very tired and the long ordeal of the day, so I went to her spare bedroom, fell into bed, and cashed in my chips.

At 2 A.M. I was awakened by someone shaking me. I looked up and there stood my friend, Sam Butcher. He said, "Wake up Lowell, the whole world is looking for you. I figured this is where you might come and I came to get you. I'm going to hide you out in one of my cabins in the woods."

So we drove out to his cabin. He gave me the keys, and said he would be back in an hour or so. Then he drove off. Later, Sam came back with some groceries and toothpaste, soap, and other toiletries I might need. I always knew Sam was a good friend, but, to drive all the way back to Carthage and go to a grocery store in the middle of the night, was going way beyond the call of duty. He had also told his high security guards to stop and one that tried to enter his property.

He felt like I did, that at any minute a van would pull up and little men in white suits would come and take me away! Their coming to take me away, Ho! Ho!

Heather did get in touch with Charlie and the rest of the family to let them know I was okay, but, that I just wanted to stay there and try to get myself back together.

When I burned my studio the news went out all over the country on the Associated Press wire. If I had done it for a publicity stunt I couldn't have done a better job than if I had cut off my ear.

Charlie got hundreds of letters from all over the country from concerned friends and collectors who were worries about me and my condition. I read those letters over and over. They were my therapy. I didn't listen to the radio or watch television during the two months I stayed in that cabin. Sam made sure I had plenty of food, and Charlie brought me the mail.

Finally I knew I was on the road to recovery, so I went home to see the damage to my studio. Later, I found out a neighbor, Garland Green, had had seen the fire at my studio and used a garden hose trying to contain the fire until the fire department got the rest of the fire out. The outside structure of my studio was still standing, other than the firemen breaking out the windows, but, when I stepped inside, it was a different story.

What a burned and charred mess! I had all my favorite possessions in that building. Forty years of chicken collecting was in there, burned beyond recognition. Almost all my paintings were gone, plus my Favorite paintings by other artists, and gifts from friends. All gone!

After a few days of being home I got a shovel and a wheelbarrow and tried to bring myself to scoop out the rubble, but I couldn't bear to scoop out all those memories. I couldn't do it for a very, very long time. It was just too sad. Finally, a friend sis it for me. We dumped all the rubble into nearby sheds, for I could see some items might have survived the fire and I wanted a closer look before destroying them completely. Then, we started tearing out the charred walls and fixtures. I stripped it to the bare walls. Then came the job of restoration.

After my carpenters put in new insulation, we re-sheet rocked her, built new cabinets and put a fresh coat of paint on everything. Now came the slow process of going through my possessions in the adjoining sheds to see if anything could be salvaged. The water from the fire department hoses had destroyed everything the fire had missed. I tried as best I could, to pick out each piece, clean it, and decide if it was worth saving.

What a sad process! My chicken collection was gone; not, I'm not talking little ceramic salt and pepper things or El Cheapo kitchen related items with chickens on them. I'm talking about beautiful wood carvings, fine porcelain chickens, antique chickens, and chicken related antiques such as advertising signs.

I sat in those sheds for days, looking at each charred piece, reminiscing about where I had acquired it or who gave it to me. I went through the remains of stacks of paintings that I had started, many of them I had finished. There didn't seem to be anything left as I looked through all those charred remains, except, memories.

Then I took a shovel and scooped out all the bits and pieces of ceramic, glass, porcelain, paper and charred wood, dug a big hole near my rebuilt studio and buried all of it.

Next came the digging through my art supplies to see if anything was salvageable. Other than a little smoke damage, every bit of my art supplies were untouched by fire and water. The turpentine, and all my different oils and oil paints, none had exploded or caught fire. Even the blank canvases and all my brushes were saved. They must have been behind a door or on shelves that had something in front of them, for they were saved. After a restocked the shelves with my old art supplies I couldn't find anything I needed to go to the art supply store and replace.

As I sat there in the middle of my studio, I looked around and started thinking about it all. Here it was, all my possessions were gone, all of them; but on the other hand all my art supplies were still intact maybe a little smoke damage, but other than that, brand new.

The more I thought about it, the more it dawned on me it was like the Lord telling me, "Lowell, I gave you a talent and you ain't goin' to waste it!"

# Chapter 8

**THE FARM CLUB:**

This chapter should have no interest for you, unless you are, or have been a club member.

From the very beginning, I didn't want to use the name Lowell Davis, it just seemed to vain. I wanted the line and the club, called FoxFire Farm, after an experience I had in the Air Force, flying in a thunder storm over the North Sea, out of Norway. There was also another time I had an experience with foxfire, when I was a little kid near the original Red Oak, during a hail storm. And, too, Schmid liked the name.

After we had used the name FoxFire Farm on my figurine line for several years, we were named in a law suit that was settled out of court. Not only did Schmid pay a lot of money to settle the suit, we also had to take the name Foxfire Farm off all the products and boxes. Now, we needed a new name. Schmid wanted to use the name Lowell Davis, but I was still reluctant. However, Schmid was gun shy about using any other name after the law suit.

When the Farm Club Started, it too, had been called the FoxFire Farm Club. At the club's birth, I was writing and illustrating the entire FoxFire Farm Gazette. I wanted it to be a fun thing, and also for it to be commercially free, however, I was on the road so much I couldn't keep doing it all myself. So, Schmid took over the publication of the Gazette and it was written and published in their home office in Randolph, Massachusetts.

Finally I just baled out of the Club. The only thing I had to do with the club was to provide Red Oak II for the annual farm club gathering.

When I saw that Schmid was going bankrupt, I wrote a letter to my collectors to explain what was going on, but the had placed a gag order on me and that was a real "No No." Schmid wouldn't go for a letter to inform collectors about anything. So, that's why I had to leave all the collectors in the blind. I was not allowed to communicate with them. The Farm Club, along with everything else, went into bankruptcy court. That's when Jerry Truman told me he wanted to buy the Lowell Davis Farm Club.

On several different occasions I advised Jerry not to buy the club. It was my thought that the Farm Club should be allowed to die with dignity and let all the Lowell Davis Border Fine Arts figurine series come to an end. The collectors who were always excited about the pieces that had been created under the highest standards of quality in casting and painting would still be able to find, buy and trade them, but my art career was an end of an era and moving in new directions.

It was time now to get on with another aspect of my career and into another art medium. Let the old line be no more.

There would be no more Border Fine Arts pieces produced, That way, the Border Fine Arts line might have a good chance on the secondary market. It would belike a fine antique. If a few new pieces kept dribbling onto the market it would only keep the secondary market confused, but I found Jerry was a difficult man to persuade to do anything, other than his own way. Jerry and I were like oil and water.

I really don't want to say anything bad about Jerry, so what I am going to say is about business men in general and their way of thinking versus an artist's way of thinking. I kept trying to work with business men but I just didn't understand them. Now I understand.

If I were to give advice to a young artist that happened to have an artist's brain, it would be to try and keep third parties out from between you and your collectors. However, finally, against my better judgment, I agreed to Jerry buying the Lowell Davis Farm Club from Schmid, and move it across from the Red Oak II General Store.
It would be housed in my grandfather's blacksmith's shop. I also agreed to do a give-away club figurine for anyone joining the club, plus I would do a club figurine once a year. In addition the these two pieces, I offered to sculpt two more Border Fine Arts pieces each year if Jerry would, in turn, let club members know that I was alive and well and am now happily employed with the ERTL Toy Company in Dyersville, Iowa. Also, we agreed that through the Lowell Davis Farm Club Gazette he would continue to keep my old collectors abreast of new introductions and update them on my new adventures. Well, Jerry agreed, and he did run something in the first Gazette published in its new home. But then something happened between Jerry and Ertl. A disagreement of some kind, after that, not one mention of Ertl over the next couple of years.

Jerry never published any Ertl related brochures, magazine articles, or anything about Ertl and me working together.

I kept my end of the bargain with Jerry and I continued to supply him with new figurine ideas and sculptures. During the next two years I kept trying to tell Jerry, "Hey man, Keep up with your part of the bargain." Jerry always had the same answer, "Well, Ertl made me mad." And I always replied, "That might be so, Jerry, but the deal was between Lowell Davis and Ertl, not Jerry Truman and Ertl."

Many times I begged Jerry to change his ways and let me contact Lowell Davis Collectors for I felt I had some right to communicate with my collectors after all those years on the road promoting the club. Wrong again, according to Jerry.

I have only received two letters from thousands of collectors during those past years that Jerry was in charge of the Lowell Davis Farm Club. I guess the reason I got those two letters is they were telling me how great the last years Farm Event was that Jerry had put on. Other than that, not even a Christmas card from any of my collectors.

An ex-employee of the Farm Club to me that Jerry had trashed all communication between my club members and me. They told me Jerry sent out letters to some of my collectors and that we, he and I, were going into a joint venture with figurines and they were going to be sold in three hundred gift shops across the country.

This is in direct violation of the very contract Jerry helped put together with Ertl. Ertl then told me that it was either Jerry Truman or them! They said I was to have Jerry take the name Lowell Davis off the Lowell Davis Farm Club. I told Ertl I completely agreed. I said the club wasn't going the way I had hoped it would, and I had no say at all in my own Lowell Davis Farm Club.

I had never been able to get my point across verbally to Jerry, so there was no point in trying to talk to him about Ertl he said.

So, I wrote Jerry a letter and said he was welcome to keep the Farm Club in my Blacksmith's shop and continue doing business as usual, but he was to take the Lowell Davis off the Farm Club, however, he could keep the name "Farm Club." Jerry exploded!

Now, Jerry is a good man in a lot of ways, but you don't tell Jerry Truman, "NO" or what he can or can't do with my name. Not only did Jerry pull out of the Blacksmith shop, he also pulled all his merchandise out of the General Store and put his house in Red Oak II up for sale. Once it was sold, he left Red Oak II.

All this was very unfortunate as Jerry and I had been best friends for many years. We've had lots of good times on the road together, but Jerry and I are oil and water. He's a numbers man and thinks with one side of his brain and, well, I think off the other side.

I want to thank Jerry for those earlier years when only friendship was involved. There is a long list of memories I never want to forget.

Now, I have always been a collector and the one thing I collected more than chickens was farm related toys. Especially toy tractors, antique and new. Ever since I was a kid, I loved Ertl farm toy. After Schmid's bankruptcy I was at a crossroads in my life. I didn't know where I was going with my career. I knew Enesco was a great distributor and a good company to work for, but the thought of me working for Ertl Toys was even more appealing.

My toy tractor collection was missing something. Ertl toys were well executed and well built. Quality wise, it was the best on today's market.

The more I thought about getting connected with Ertl toys the more appealing it became to get on the Ertl team. I could just see my cold cast porcelain figurines combined with the beautiful Ertl die cast tractors, cars, and trucks. Although Ertl products were well done and beautiful, they kinda just sat there on the shelf. They said nothing, did nothing. They needed life. They needed to breathe.

That's where I knew I could come in. I worked feverishly for the next few months designing a Lowell Davis-Ertl look. When I had finally designed enough products I went to Dyersville to show Ertl how I thought Ertl and I could make beautiful music together.

Ertl was very receptive and loved my new concept, so we signed a contract. In my career it has been a long climb up the ladder to finally sign with a great company like Ertl. The long ladder that I have climbed has had a lot of prestigious rungs like Kaiser Porcelain Company of Germany, distributors like Ebbling & Ruess and Schmid, the Danbury Mint, Pelican Press-Publishers of my book on chickens, puzzles by Hallmark, Louisville Pottery, Chillmark Pewter, Anri Woodcarvings of Italy, and the list goes on.

Now I feel with Ertl, I am on the top rung of the ladder. You can't go any higher. I'm not with Ertl to try to replace Border Fine Arts, that had its own time period, its own art, its own collectors. With Ertl, I'm singing a new song, and in no way should that song be compared to Border Fine Arts.

Ertl has more than sixty thousand outlets, farm and implement dealers that dot our vast countryside. As you drive around the country you see many John Deere dealerships and almost all of those dealerships handle Ertl toy replicas of tractors and implements they sell. So, that's where I am now. With Ertl in those dealerships. I couldn't be happier.

I have a different collector base and they have never heard of Border Fine Arts, but those collectors are becoming familiar and are collecting the name Ertl-Lowell Davis.

When someone starts collecting your name and your work they want to know more about the artist and find out what the artist has done in the past. When these collectors go back into my past they will find all those wonderful little farm animals that I created for Border Fine Arts. The only problem is, they can no longer go into a gift shop in their neighborhood and purchase them.

The only folks who have those little figurines is YOU! The collectors. If the new collectors wants to get on board and own any of those old pieces, they will have to buy then from a Border Fine Arts collector, YOU!

This is what I have always wanted. To bring out new collectors to create and revive interest in my figurines. Keeping Border Fine Arts collection a good investment. Not like the Farm Club was trying to do by making a couple Border Fine Arts pieces each year. This keeps the Border Fine Arts secondary market confused. The introduction of all my new Ertl collectors to the Border Fine Arts collections is already working. Many new collectors are now trying to locate people with B.F.A. pieces to see if they would be interested in selling any of them. This should start a new and exciting movement back to the Border Fine Arts figurines.

## Chapter 9

**The Cabin in the Ozarks**

**FINDING MY NICHE**:

Many people are curious about what happened at Red Oak II. Well, at this time no one is more curious than I am about what is happening at Red Oak II. As I was building the small community it was only supposed to be an art statement and a place where my club members could come and spend the night, if there were driving through "our neck of the woods."

Red Oak II was also a place the club could hold it's annual farm gathering. It was mainly for collectors. After all, it was their own town. It had only been a few years earlier that we had opened it to the public.

Regretfully, Jerry Truman, who was manager of Red Oak II at the time decided to make some of my buildings into shops, whereby people would rent the buildings and sell their wares. The timing, to begin this sort of venture was terrible. We didn't advertise to speak of, so there just wasn't enough traffic going through Red Oak II to support any of the vendors. All of them had a difficult time keeping their heads above water. It was too sad for me, getting people's hopes up, them quitting their jobs and coming out to Red Oak II to try to make a living.

After all those broken dreams the only business I wanted to open in Red Oak II was the Black Hen Pub and Grill., operated by me and my family. I don't believe we ever enjoyed anything as much as the pub; however, It demanded all of our time. I wasn't getting any painting done.

After about a year and a half, I thought, "What is more profitable, being a bartender or being an artist?" Artist, Right?, so we closed the doors to the pub and maybe, someday, someone else will want to run it. But it ain't gonna be me!

Other than the pub, the church, and the school house, Red Oak II is a ghost town. I guess Red Oak has always been a ghost town, only it had been a manicured ghost town. All I ever wanted was that it support itself financially, but unfortunately that did not happen.

At one time every building, every truck, car, and wagon in Red Oak II was in mint condition, but that was when Schmid was going great guns and I could afford to keep sinking money in Red Oak II. But after taking the financial blood bath from the Schmid disaster, there was no money coming in to me personally and that meant Red Oak II could no longer be maintained, much less have new construction. It is sad to see the slow deterioration of Red Oak II. All the buildings needed to be painted. Things were falling apart but if it turns into a falling down ghost town, then so be it. It will still be my work of and people can still come out and walk around and make themselves at home.

Some people ask, "Well, Lowell, now that you are with Ertl, can't you use some of that money for Red Oak's upkeep?"

"Well, yes, I guess I could. But my family and my farm need upkeep too, and from now on, that's where my attention is going to be. Red Oak II was fun to build and it gave a lot of people jobs, but now all Red Oak II represents is work." Red Oak II has drained me mentally, physically, and financially.

I want to personally thank those thousands of people who have given to and traded at Red Oak II.

I think its demise can be contributed to the takers and not the givers, and the folks who live within just a few miles of here, and have not been out to see the creation that is Red Oak II.

What does an artist have to do to get out of their Lazy Boys and turn off the television with its spectator sports? I don't know what it takes. All I know is that Charlie and I gave it our best shot and we gave up.

Charlie and our three daughters, April, Heather and Wren have always loved the Ozark Mountain streams about fifty miles south of Carthage.

Ever summer weekend if any of them got a chance to get away, they would head south and spend a summer day on those beautiful rivers. They would canoe, swim, and just goof off on the river.

Often, if they had more than a day, they would rent a room at the Arthur Murray Hotel in Noel, Missoura. They really loved the Arthur Murray, as the balcony of the hotel hung out over the beautiful Elk River. Then, something happened that Charlie will never forget, nor will I! It was September, 1997, and Charlie and the three girls packed up and headed to the Arthur Murray.

That summer, I had noticed all of them looking through real estate ads, and they told me when we were financially able, they wanted to buy a lot on the river and build a cabin, but I never thought much more about it.

This particular weekend all my girls had gone to Noel canoeing for a couple of days. I had stayed home to help out at the pub. Saturday afternoon, Sam Butcher called and asked if I was busy? "No," I said, "come on out."

Sam drove up in my barn lot and I walked out to his car to greet him. He said for me to get in because he wanted to just drive around and talk. That was fine with me because I was anxious to show Sam my two latest life size junk iron sculptures, "The Crapduster" and "A poor man has poor ways." Both are located just east of Carthage on Highway 96.

Sam and I hadn't seen each other for several months. I told him about the art projects I had been involved in and then it was his turn to talk. Sam said, "Lowell, I always tithe at least 10% of my earnings to some organization, or someone in need." He went on the say he just concluded a big business deal and he didn't know who to give the $10,000.00 to. The 10% tithe from his business deal.

He said he had prayed about it over and over. He had a list of organizations, churches, and building funds to which he donated, but he said the more he prayed about it, the name "Lowell Davis" kept coming up. Then he said, "Now, Lowell, I don't know what you need $10,000.00 dollars for. It might be for Red Oak II, it might be for advertising, or it just might be for you or your family. I don't know. All I know is the Lord has directed me to you. So, here's a check for $10,000.00 dollars.

"Sam, I've always appreciated the financial support you have given to Red Oak II, but I'm not going to stick another dime into Red Oak II, although it can sure use the money. And if I'm not going to put anymore money into it, then I don't think you should either." Sam said, "Well, Lowell, when I pray over these donations, the Lord never steers me wrong. Maybe it's for you personally. Do you need a vacation, or something like that."

Again, I said, "Sam, I appreciate that very much., but, I'm making ends meet, barely! But I am making it. I think you should just go back home and pray over it again because this time it looks like the Lord led you astray."

I thanked him again for the offer, but before he drove off, he asked me to come have lunch with him the next day at Precious Moments.

About dusk, that same day, Charlie came home from the canoe trip, all excited, and tells me she and April had just bought the cutest little cabin overlooking a river in the Ozarks.

I said, "YOU DID WHAT?"

Then she rattled off all the wonderful features about the cabin, and finally said, "Well, I did it for you and for is. We need to get away from this monster (Red Oak II and the Farm) we've created at least a couple of days or nights a week."

Then, I began hollering at her, "You mean you bought a house without even asking your husband about it. Now, Charlie, I've never complained about you buying antiques, or new clothes, or something. You know I have no restrictions on you, BUT A HOUSE? We don't have the money, taking into consideration there's no money coming in from Schmid since the bankruptcy, and I know Ertl is looking good, but that's still in the future. We are barely making it now" Finally, I got around to asking, "How much did you pay down?" Charlie replied, in her quiet little voice, all the time batting her eyes at me, "$10,000.00."

'TEN THOUSAND DOLLARS? WHERE IN THE HELL ARE WE EVER GOING TO COME UP WITH $10,000 DOLLARS?" Then I really went into a rage. I didn't throw anything or break anything but I used up my years quota of profanity the next couple of hours.

I was s mad I was kickin' dogs.

All this time I was yelling at her and calling her every name except a white woman, and she'd just let my words fall like water off a duck's back. She just kept smiling and sliding in the words, "I did it for you, too!" and the more she smiled when I was so angry, the madder it made me.

It was late in the night before I calmed down enough to go to bed. I went to sleep and woke at 2 A.M. I couldn't go back to sleep from thinking about her doing such a thing. Finally, I got out of bed, put on my clothes and drove down to the Flyin' W and bought myself a pint of tequila, then I went home and downed it. I passed out and woke up the next morning with this humongous hangover. I hadn't been anywhere near this shape since that last night in Atlanta, twenty six years earlier.

I lie there in the bed trying to get my huge head off my pillow. I decided just to lie there and stay mad for the rest of the day, but the more I thought about it and after getting over the original shock, I got to thinking, "You know Lowell, Charlie has done everything that you've wanted to do. Living my dreams, working her fingers to the bone every day for Red Oak II and she never received one dime's pay from Red Oak II for all her effort. She's been living my dreams for the past 25 years and I guess now it's my turn to spend the next twenty five years of our marriage doing what Charlie wants to do" I decided.

I got out of bed and went down stairs to the kitchen where Charlie was having her fifteenth cup of morning coffee to give her a kick-start, and said, "Sweet, I'm sorry for my reaction yesterday. It's that you just caught me off guard. But, if it's the cabin you and the girls want, I'll figure out where we can come up with the down payment." But I had to ask, "By the way, Charlie, I do have one little bitty question. I know you said the reason you made that down payment before you asked me about it was that cabins on the river always sell as soon as they are listed and that cabin was so perfect, you were afraid it would sell at any moment, but what was the real reason?" I asked.

"Let me fix you a great breakfast and after breakfast let me take you down there and I'll show you the cabin," then added, "and in answer to your question, the real reason I didn't ask you first was because I knew you would say, NO!"

"Thank you," I said, "but the cabin will be for you and the girls. I really don't care to have anything to do with it. Maybe I'll go down with you a couple of times a year, but that's it. I never, never ever told you , Charlie, that I wanted a cabin overlooking the river. In fact I NEVER SAID I wanted a cabin anywhere. I am perfectly content right here on the farm."

Then she said, "Come on sour puss, Let's go down and let me show you our new cabin."

Reluctantly I agreed. On the drive down she kept rattling on and on about how great it was going to be. After we got to the cabin, she started showing me all its features. We waded in the creek behind the cabin and sat on the opposite bank of the creek and she said, "Right over there is where you could build your new "fire proof" studio. Then, maybe you could get come painting done."

All the time she's telling me about this cabin, she's throwing key words, "You need this too, Lowell;" "You really need this on your life right now." And "Don't you just love it?"

The longer I sat there on that creek bank, looking back at the cabin and spot where I could build a new studio, the better it seemed. It even dawned on me that maybe I di dneed to get away a couple days a week.

Then, I got up, popped Charlie on the rear and said, "Come on Sweet. We need to get back to the farm and figure out where we are going to come up with $10,000 dollars to cover that hot check you just wrote to the real estate company." On the drive home, I tild her the story about Sam Butcher coming out. At the very time she was at the real estate office writing that hot check for $10,000 dollars, Sam was trying to give me $10,000.00 to go on a vacation. I guess everyone could tell by my stress and my health, I needed a get-a-way. That was, everyone but me.

Then I told Charlie, "In no way an I going to back out on my good friend Sam, and say that I would take the money." We continued to talk about ways we come up with the money that fast. Well, the next day came around and we still hadn't figured out how to come up with the money. If nothing else, I guessed we could take out a loan, but I didn't build Red Oak II with borrowed money and I didn't want to start borrowing now.

Charlie suggested I might get an advance from Ertl on my royalties. "No," I said to that idea. I didn't want to get in the habit of borrowing money from a new company that I had just started with.

I told Charlie I had a lunch appointment with Sam, and later, over lunch, I told Sam the story about what Charlie had done. Sam jumps up out of his seat and shouted, "I knew it! I knew it! The Lord didn't lead me astray after all!" Then Sam demanded that I accept the money to make the down payment on the cabin on the river.

I said, "Look Sam, I didn't mind you, or anyone else giving money to Red Oak II. I've always accepted money in the past, but Sam," I explained, "This is a different deal. This is a personal financial problem and I've never ever wanted to use our friendship to receive money from you. But, I will tell you the one way I would take the money and that is if I could trade it out with my originals." We shook hands and he wrote me out a check for the down payment on the cabin.

I left and told Sam I would be right back. I hurried home and picked up a large painting of Red Oak II in the snow, titled "The Backsliders" and if I have ever painted my masterpiece, this was it. I never wanted to sell it, but now I decided to give it to Sam, to say, "Thank you. Thanks again Sam."

With Ertl doing great, I can sit now in my new studio, over looking an Ozark mountain stream, doing what I love most to do. Painting, with Charlie on the back porch, just a swingin'.

# Chapter 10

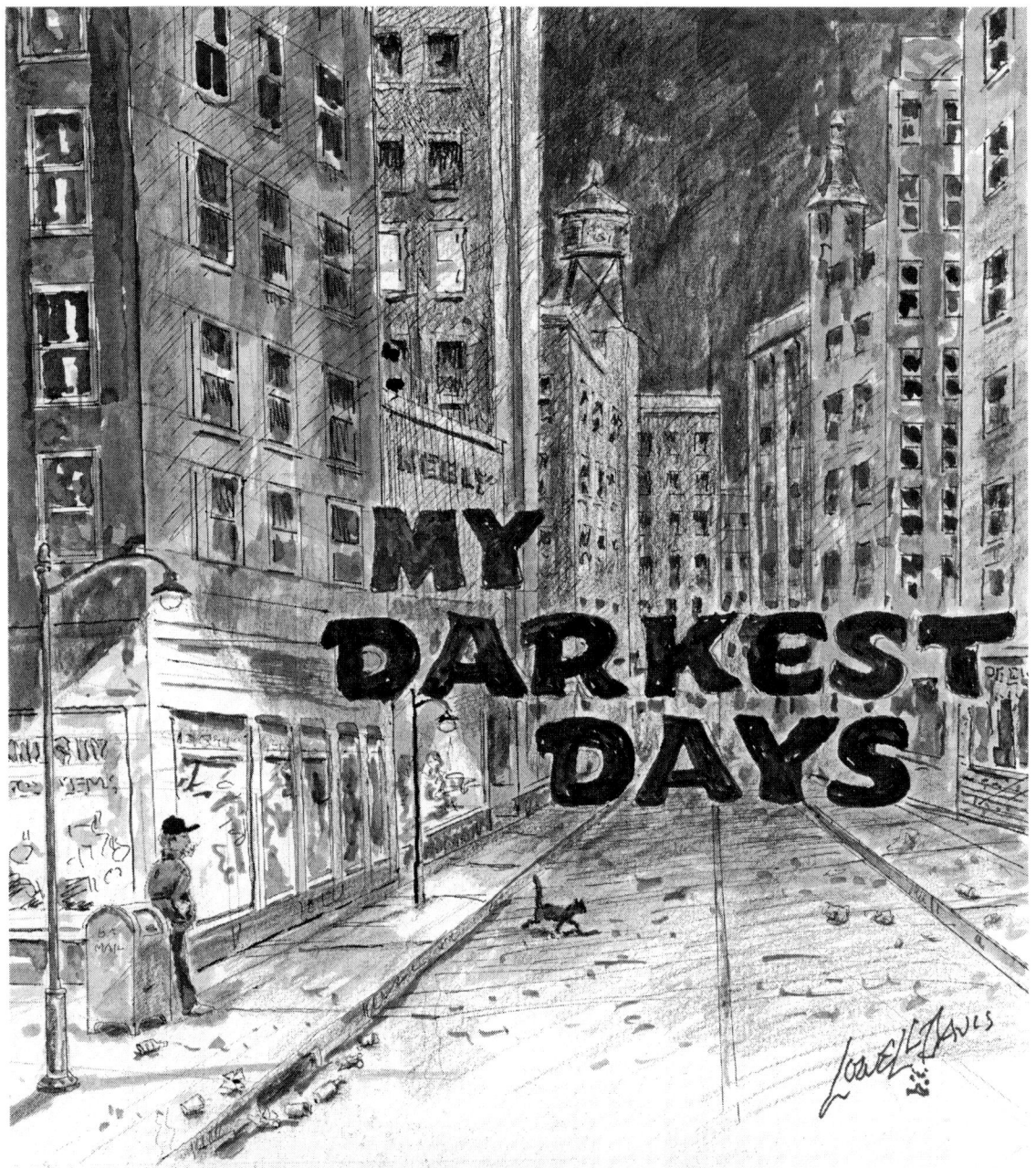

**Cold and all alone in Chicago**

**MY DARKEST DAYS:**

Well, it all sounds like a fairy tale ending, but try as I may, our marriage kept heading south, and all the king's horses and all the king's men, plus a lot of prayers couldn't get or marriage back together again. I soon found out why I needed that cabin so much. Because

Charlie kicked my out of the farm house, so I spent the next four years on one hell of a pity party. I didn't do any painting during that time. I mostly sat in an overstuffed chair in the dark thinking I could find the answer at the bottle of a bottle of Jack Daniels.

Like most men in their early years, I did my share of bar hopping and while in the Air Force in England and Europe, I went from bar to bar with "the boys". Then, of course, I did some sorrow drowning during the split with Nancy. When I met Charlie, I had just finished several days of drinking myself into a stooper. But after meeting Charlie and finding my faith, I had stopped drinking completely, so while on this binge hugging that bottle of Jack Daniels had a double effect on me. I'm not what you would call a drinking man. The only time I drank was when I was going through divorces. The only thing I learned from alcohol is that it always lies to you.

After a few years of trying to drown my marital problems I decided to pray them away. I prayed several times a day to get my marriage back together. Out of all that praying during my life this was the only prayer that I kept praying that never came true. I couldn't figure out why it wasn't answered. A couple of years later I found out why. The Lord had something much better in store for me.

I did a lot of canoeing during those four years. I think I have canoed every creek the Ozark Mountains have to offer. I even knew the rivers so well that I could float them in the moonlight, which I did. After a couple of years of that I realized a man can only do so much canoeing.

It was about this time that Charlie had applied with American Airlines for a position as a flight hostess. Not surprisingly, she was accepted and she loaded up her Grand Cherokee and left to go to Dallas, Texas for training, never to return to Red Oak II or the Foxfire Farm, except occasionally coming home to pick up items to decorate her new apartment in Chicago, Illinois. Her first assignment was flying out of O' Hare International Airport in Chicago.

We had very little communication over the next few months after she left flight hostess classes and the beginning of her new career. She came to Foxfire Farm during Thanksgiving and wanted me to help her move her furniture and items to decorate her new apartment. Our son Jeb was home on leave from the Air Force, and wanted to rent a U-Haul and assist in the drive to Chicago. Our conversation was pleasant, but cool on the drive.

We got to her apartment and unloaded the U-Haul. She and I left Jeb at the apartment and we drove a few blocks to find a backstreet parking lot. Walking back to her apartment, I said the wrong thing to her. I said, "Do you mean, Charlie, you are trading our farm, our Red Oak II, and our family for a two bedroom apartment on the 32$^{nd}$ floor in downtown Chicago?" Well, that really pissed her off and she took off running down the dark street and out of site.

There I was, out in the cold on the dark backstreets of Chicago. I am petrified of big cities, period! But I had no idea of which direction to go or where her new apartment was. I could find my way back to the parking lot, but she had the keys. On that cold November night, not knowing where I was or how to find the apartment, I finally got it through my thick skull that any woman that would do this to me… It was just wishful thinking on my part that we could ever get out marriage back together and a divorce was imminent.

It seemed like hours, me standing on that corner like a lost pup trying to figure out what I was going to do, but about twenty minutes later Jeb came looking for me and I followed him back to her apartment. Upon arriving I was more hurt than angry, It was then that she told me that her father had paid for her apartment on a fifteen year note. And she was planning on staying with American Airlines until she could retire in fifteen years. Putting two and two together, even I could figure this marriage was ended. We both agreed that we were divorced and all that was left was lawyers and signing divorce papers. It was a long silent drive back to Missouri with Jeb that night. As soon as I arrived at the farm, I took my wedding ring off and threw it in the duck pond. I heard it go "kerplunk" as it hit the water and sank to the bottom where it still lays. I know most people handle divorces badly, especially if they are the ones on the receiving end. But if there was a contest on bad losers I would have come home with the Blue Ribbon.

Now that Charlie had moved out of the farmhouse, I was allowed to move back in. I was married to Charlie for thirty years and as I always say, they were the best fifteen years of my life. I spent the next few months putting the divorce together and sinking lower and lower into my depression.

# Chapter 11

**Love at First sight!**

## ROSE, THE NEW BEGINNING:

I must have looked like walking death when my friend Sam Butcher came home from the Philippines for the Christmas holidays. He invited me out to dinner on Christmas Eve and without my telling everything about my problems he gathered by my appearance that I was on the bottom. The next day, Christmas, Sam again drives up into my barn lot. He hurriedly runs to the back door of the Farmhouse just as I was going out to greet him and he says to me, "Lowell, I want to give you a Christmas present. An all expenses paid trip to the Philippines. The land of the friendly people." Well, two weeks later I'm in Manila, with Sam. To help me get out of my slump he had made plans to entertain me for the next couple of weeks. First of all he wanted to take me to his new get-away on an island forty five minutes flight from Manila.

Festivals were in full swing in every town and province in the Philippines. I was coming out of my depression quickly with all the fun touring and being with all those happy people of Kalibo on this little island. It ain't no wonder why Sam loves this place so much. The

Philippines might be one of the most poverty-ridden countries, but the people are the most friendliest and happiest. Filipinos do not simply provide their guests with a place to rest or offer them food. They give the very best they have, even to all they have. This warm effusive brand of hospitality is what distinguishes the Philippine people from all others. I cried when we left and couldn't talk for the next several miles thinking about all those beautiful people that were friends that Sam had introduced me to.

We rented a car and drove through this giant province with little villages, mountains, and rice patties. We arrived at the southern end of the island to the capital of the province, Iloilo City. Again, when we arrives, Sam had the Red Carpet laid out for me. Our mutual friend JoJo took the day off and showed me all the sights of this unique town. The next day we caught a flight back to Manila. After only three days my pity-party was just disappearing and I was getting my sea-legs back under me.

When we arrived back in Manila, the first thing Sam wanted to do was to take me to his favorite restaurant. It is a Five Star Chinese restaurant in downtown Manila. It was while we were having lunch that Sam introduced me to the manager. Beings Sam was a regular the manager sat at our table with us. Her name was Rose. Sam saw the instant spark between us and excused himself and left Rose and me so we could talk. If there was ever "love at first sight", it was now. There in that restaurant with Rose, I turned on all my charm and had Rose eating out of my hand in no time.

Sam had told me about the great tourist area that a wealthy Philipino had reconstructed from a pre-Second World War Philippine village and farming area. I asked Rose if she could take off work and go with me to Escudero Gardens. She accepted and we spent the greatest day of my life together in the most picturesque tropical paradise I had ever seen. By the end of that fantastic day there was no doubt about it. With Rose's smile, charm, intelligence and humor, I was head over heels in love.

Sam had set big plans for him and me for the nest two weeks and a half. We had plans to go to Bataan and visit the sight of the Bataan Death March from World War II, then fly to Thailand, and all kinds of new and exciting adventures, but the next day I had to say, "Sam, I know I would really enjoy seeing and experiencing all those places, but I think I'll just stay here in Manila with Rose." And, that's what I did. Rose and I spent together every moment she was not working until it came to the sad time of leaving. I arrived back home with all the years of divorce pain going away.

Five weeks later, Sam used all his prestige in the Philippines to get rose a visa and he personally accompanied her to the United States and he personally delivered her to my door.

As if it wasn't enough for Sam to send me to the Philippines for the greatest time of my life, as if it wasn't enough for Sam to bring Rose to the "States", he gave us a grandiose wedding. A fairy tale wedding all expenses paid, at his wedding chapel on the grounds of Precious Moments.

Rose soon adapted to her new surroundings and started to spoil me rotten, which I deserved after the past dreadful years. Along with spoiling me, Rose also gave me encouragement, respect and love, which made me want to start painting again. As Sam told me, "Lowell, you are me best and dearest friend and if you go broke, the only reason will be because you don't paint." Well, paint I did. The enthusiasm came back. My adrenalin started pumping and I felt I was now painting the best that I had ever painted.

Rose and I moved into Red Oak II and settled in the Belle Starr house, which is my favorite home in Red Oak II. Since Charlie was living in Chicago and Rose and I were living in the Belle Starr house, Charlie and I gave the old farm to our daughter Wren. Life is good again, I am painting, Rose contacted a lot of my collectors and she is also going great guns selling my prints and originals on EBay.

Yes, Lowell Davis has a computer, but I still don't allow a television in the house since I threw our old one in the pond twenty five years ago. That TV floated in the duck pond for three years with it's big eye starring up at the sky until one day I took me 30_30 out there and shot it to put it out of its misery.

As happy as Rose and I were, Red Oak was growing sadder and sadder. Every building was getting rotten boards and was I desperate need of painting, love and tender care. I no longer had funds or the possibilities of all the upkeep that it takes to maintain Red Oak II.

I had been begging Charlie to let me sell Red Oak II in pieces, meaning sell a house and a business to individuals to own and do their own upkeep. But Charlie and her Father were adamant on selling Red Oak II as a whole, like to a big investment group, which I could not bring myself to do. I figured any investment group would just whore Red Oak II to death and I would have to move from my beloved Belle Starr home. I was living in the middle of my art and no matter how much money we would get for selling Red Oak II as a whole, I would not want to live anywhere else in the world except on the front porch in the summer and by the fireplace in the winter. So with this Mexican standoff between Charlie wanting to sell It as a whole and.

*There ain't no memories in First Class*

**Editor's Note: I think this might be the first wedding invitation to include past wives as well as current wife. Wives I, II, and III. This is a scan of the actual invitation painted by Lowell.**

me wanting to sell it off to individuals, seven years went by and under these conditions we were without any sale of Red Oak II. I did have a few bullshitters that wanted to buy if but both of these deals turned into nightmares

Finally, I paid to have this elaborate web site which took us three months to build. After completing this web site that Red Oak II was for sale, I told Charlie that it ran on EBay and several other channels, but to no avail. I told her I didn't get any takers, so it was then and only then she agreed to sell Red Oak II to individuals. It was not two weeks and without any for sale signs or advertising, Red Oak II was completely sold.

It was like the Lord said, "Lowell, I know what you have gone through and Red Oak II is too good to go to the ground, so I am sending you some of the greatest people on Earth to help you get her fixed up brand new again and maintain her." So, there will be a lot of excitement and expanding and adding to my metal art sculptures on the grounds.

I think the main reason it took so long for me to finish this book is because I could not come up with the last few chapters. I wanted to finish it on an upbeat note. Now, with Rose by my side and all the good property owners which have bought houses and businesses our Red Oak II and have already restored her back to its original grandeur, I have lots of folks I can dream with. I'm in hog heaven.

The Lord has blessed me with inner peace and with Rose, I am the happiest that I have ever been. I can set on my front porch, smoke my pipe and drink my coffee, pick ticks off my dogs and watch my new neighbors and friends, doing the mowing and repairing, painting and adding new and exciting buildings. With the new facelift at Red Oak II we are getting excited with the prospects of seeing all our friends in the coming Spring and we are going to be open full bore in 2006.

I ain't goin' to cal this the "The End." I'm just sayin' that I am headed out for the next adventure that life has to offer. It doesn't matter if that life's road leads me into valleys or hills, I'm just along for the ride!

Thanks for being my friends.

Lowell Davis

The Missoura Kid

December, 2005.

*There ain't no memories in First Class*

**Lowell, in his '50 Ford and dog in the back, heading for new adventures.**

OPPS, WE'RE NOT FINISHED YET! DON'T RUN OFF!

**Missoura Kid, Real Estate Mogul**

I sure hope you have enjoyed my life's story

As you know, I have sold many pieces of property within Red Oak II to private individuals. Rose and I have kept my favorite house, the Belle Starr house, and we have made this our home and residence. We also kept the Blacksmith's shop and the Birdsong.

All the new owners have rolled up their sleeves and repaired and painted their new acquisitions and have brought the back to their original beauty. In fact, they have restored them even more beautifully than I did originally.

Since they have worked so hard, I would like to introduce you to some of the new owners of Red Oak II and me new neighbors.

Tom and Carol Klinginsmith, long time friend and local Attorney-at-Law, has purchased the beautifully restored Garfield-Wiley log home and have made it a lovable and comfortable residence.

Larry Sernyk, one of my most avid collectors over the years and has collected at least three of every figurine that I ever sculpted throughout me career. These include Kaiser Porcelain, Ertl, Schmid, Louisville Pottery as well as bronzes. Larry has purchased the General Store to house his collection and will put these pieces on display so that other collectors and visitors may view the many lines of sculptures.

Larry and Lois Frickenschmidt have purchased several buildings. Larry's father Elmer Frickenschmidt had a rural milk run in this neck of the woods for many years and Larry bought the Feed Store in which he plans to put in a dairy and feed museum as a tribute to his father. Larry and Lois have also bought the Marshall's Office and Marshall Hooker's cabin and have cut no corners in the cost of renovating these cute little buildings and they will pay tribute to Marshall Hooker by making these into a museum. They have also acquired the Town Hall, The Wren House, the mule barn as well as the wagon and tractor shed which has also been restored.

Lois has completely restored and painted the Wren House into a bed and breakfast as cute as any doll house. Their plans for the Town Hall will be for a meeting and gathering place. It will also have a loom and will hold quilting bees. They have decorated it with wonderful antiques.

The Frickenschmidt's have also leased the Birdsong from Rose and I and intend to convert this one of a kind building into a little shop that will offer some western furniture and trappings, original oil paintings and prints by local artists as well as selected antiques.

*There ain't no memories in First Class*

Larry and Lois Frickenschmidt have recently purchased the Black Hen Restaurant. An early autumn re-opening is being planned following some renovations. Watch for a few changes and good food on the horizon. Whenever Larry is doing a project, count on it being done right with a solid result!

I wish to also introduce you to Tim and Mary Darch, or as we affectionately call them, Brother Tim and Sister Mary. They have bought the School the Schoolmarm's House, the Phillips 66 gas station, the two Acorn Cabins, and the Salem Church.

The Schoolmarm's house is also being renovated into a lovely bed and breakfast. Tim also has put the Salem Church to good use by providing the locals with a lovely service on Sunday evenings when he preaches, They will also be renting the church out for weddings.

Red Oak II is in the process of restoring a beautiful Fire Station and also Red Oak II has gotten her own wonderfully restored old wooden water tower, plus much, much more.... Well, it would be much easier for y'all just to come by and see these fine folks in the Spring of '06.

The welcome mat is always out! You won't be disappointed.

*Lowell Davis*